Pre-publication REVIEWS, COMMENTARIES, EVALUATIONS . . .

"**R**ichard Kagan's *Real Life Heroes* is a real lifesaver for therapists searching to find helpful techniques to work with children who have experienced multiple traumas. Expressive, multisensory, creative methods are utilized to help children express feelings about their past traumatic experiences. The hero concept helps youth to visualize their strengths and to think in terms of future success. The Making Things Better chapter provides helpful strategies to help children regulate their feelings. The ABC's of Trauma and the Hero's Challenge help children to look at the beliefs and actions that are keeping them stuck and the actions they can take to feel successful. This book is a must-have for every therapist or psychologist who works with traumatized children."

—**Arlene Fisher, MA, LPC, LMFT**
Director, Child Welfare Services,
DePelchin Children's Center

"**T**he *Real Life Heroes* practitioner's manual is an excellent resource and supplement to the *Real Life Heroes* workbook. The manual steps beyond a simple expansion on the exercises contained within the workbook, offering information on topics such as supporting children and families on their journey, assessment of child and system needs, engagement of 'caring adults,' pacing of treatment, and trouble-shooting, with recognition of the real-world dilemmas often facing clinicians working with this complicated population. Prominent throughout the manual is a tone of respect for the children, families, and care giving systems impacted by complex trauma."

—**Margaret E. Blaustein, PhD**
Director of Training and Education,
The Trauma Center at JRI

"**R**eal Life Heroes is a unique and highly creative approach to helping children and parents recover from trauma. It is inspiring for therapists as well as for the children and families they are helping. The book and program offer a wonderful set of paths with which people of all ages can rediscover the hero in themselves and each other."

—**Julian D. Ford, PhD,**
Associate Professor and Director,
Center for Trauma Response, Recovery,
and Preparedness (CTRP), Department of Psychiatry,
University of Connecticut Health Center

Real Life Heroes
Practitioner's Manual

The Haworth Press®
Maltreatment, Trauma, and Interpersonal Aggression
Robert A. Geffner
Senior Editor

Real Life Heroes
Practitioner's Manual

Richard Kagan, PhD

The Haworth Press, Inc.
New York

For more information on this book or to order, visit
http://www.haworthpress.com/store/product.asp?sku=5639

or call 1-800-HAWORTH (800-429-6784) in the United States and Canada
or (607) 722-5857 outside the United States and Canada

or contact orders@HaworthPress.com

The Haworth Press, Inc., 10 Alice Street, Binghamton, NY 13904-1580.

PUBLISHER'S NOTE
The development, preparation, and publication of this work has been undertaken with great care. However, the Publisher, employees, editors, and agents of The Haworth Press are not responsible for any errors contained herein or for consequences that may ensue from use of materials or information contained in this work. The Haworth Press is committed to the dissemination of ideas and information according to the highest standards of intellectual freedom and the free exchange of ideas. Statements made and opinions expressed in this publication do not necessarily reflect the views of the Publisher, Directors, management, or staff of The Haworth Press, Inc., or an endorsement by them.

Identities and circumstances of individuals discussed in this book have been changed to protect confidentiality.

Portions of the *TARGET Facilitator Guide for Adolescents* Copyright © 2001-2006, created under the direction of Dr. Julian Ford, are used with the permission of the University of Connecticut Health Center.

Library of Congress Cataloging-in-Publication Data

Kagan, Richard.
    Real life heroes : practitioner's manual / Richard Kagan.
        p. ; cm.
    Includes bibliographical references.
    ISBN: 978-0-7890-2952-2 (soft : alk. paper)
    1. Abused children—Rehabilitation—Handbooks, manuals, etc. 2. Psychic trauma in children—Treatment—Handbooks, manuals, etc. 3. Creation (Literary, artistic, etc.)—Therapeutic use—Handbooks, manuals, etc. I. Title.
    [DNLM: 1. Stress Disorders, Traumatic—therapy. 2. Child Abuse—therapy. 3. Child. 4. Intergenerational Relations. 5. Psychotherapy—methods. WM 172 K118r 2007]
RJ507.A29K34 2007
618.92'8521—dc22
                                                                                    2007015795

To my brothers and sisters,
Carolyn, Cathy, Gina, Glenn, Jim A., Jim K.,
Laurie, Lenny, Mary, Ron, and Steve,
and in memory of
Millie Schwartz.

Life is not a problem to be solved but a mystery to be lived.

Joseph Campbell

CONTENTS

ABOUT THE AUTHOR

Richard Kagan, PhD, is Director of Psychological Services for Parsons Child and Family Center in Albany, New York, and formerly Clinical Director/Principal Investigator for Parsons Child Trauma Study Center, a community services site for the National Child Traumatic Stress Network. He is the author and co-author of six books about child and family services: *Families in Perpetual Crisis* with Shirley Schlosberg; *Turmoil to Turning Points: Building Hope for Children in Crisis Placements; Wounded Angels: Lessons from Children in Crisis; Rebuilding Attachments with Traumatized Children: Healing from Losses, Violence, Abuse, and Neglect; Real Life Heroes: A Life Story Book for Children;* and *Real Life Heroes: Practitioner's Manual.* He has also published over twenty articles, chapters, and papers on practice and research issues in trauma therapy, child welfare, foster care, adoption, professional development, program evaluation, and quality improvement in family service agencies. Dr. Kagan has worked as a consulting psychologist for county departments of social services and several child and family service agencies. Professional honors include two awards for distinguished achievement in child and family services. Dr. Kagan has been a workshop leader and keynote speaker at national and international conferences sponsored by family service agencies in the United States and Canada, and at state and regional conferences of trauma therapy, family violence, and home-based family service associations. His presentations, articles, and books highlight practical and innovative approaches that practitioners can utilize to help traumatized children and families.

Acknowledgments

This manual was adapted from *Rebuilding Attachments with Traumatized Children: Healing from Losses, Violence, Abuse, and Neglect* (The Haworth Press, 2004) and was designed as a reference and training manual for *Real Life Heroes: A Life Storybook for Children* (The Haworth Press, 2007). *Real Life Heroes* incorporates neuropsychological research (e.g., Schore, 2003; Siegel and Hartzell, 2003; van der Kolk, 2003); trauma therapies (e.g., Figley, 1989; Ford & Russo, 2006; Herman, 1992; Pynoos & Nader, 1988; Shapiro, 2001; van der Kolk, 2003); cognitive behavioral interventions (e.g., Beck, 1976; Cohen, Mannarino & Deblinger, 2003; Lazarus, 1971); and life story and narrative therapies (e.g., Freedman and Combs, 1996; Jewett, 1978; Kliman, 1996; White & Epston, 1990). The author is especially grateful to Robert Geffner, PhD, editor for The Haworth Press, for his support, inspiration, and assistance with all of the *Real Life Heroes* books.

Adaptations of this manual were based on consultations with therapists and researchers involved in studies of the *Real Life Heroes* model. The author is especially grateful to Carrie Blanchard, Julie Bouse, Melissa Brinkman, Cheryl Brown-Merrick, Amber Douglas, Laurie Gendron, Christi Hart, John Hornik, Susannah Kratz, Jennifer LeMay, Sandy Miles, Alaina Mormile, Sydney Mullin, Mary Purdy, Lynne Ross, Janice Slavik, Danielle Stokely, Peg Sutton, Marian Truax, and Heather Verkade for their recommendations and additions to this manual. Caroline Peacock and Courtney Hawkins provided valuable tips on engaging adolescents. Recommendations concerning telling the "trauma story" were enhanced by training and consultation in Trauma Focused-Cognitive Behavioral Therapy provided by Esther Deblinger through the National Child Traumatic Stress Network. Trauma psychoeducation and skill-building activities incorporated adaptations of *TARGET* and *FREEDOM* developed by Julian Ford.

Dr. Amber Douglas drafted the initial outlines for work on the first four chapters of the *Life Storybook*. Melanie Carbin and Elizabeth Power provided valuable editorial advice on shaping the manual and Marilyn Orenstein helped prepare preliminary versions. Judy Riopelle helped edit and prepare the research editions and Joann Sutton helped organize later versions for use by Parsons staff. Judy also developed the format and style for the bookmark, added graphics to multiple sections, and helped make the manual much more readable. Amy Scheele prepared the "Heroes Library" list as well as the original "Knots" (Sutton, 2004) and "Personal Power" (Purdy, 2004) "My Thermometers" (adapted from Ford, Mahoney, and Russo, 2001, and Walk, 1956). Kathy Tambasco provided graphic and word processing assistance, and Dennis Chapko resolved computer problems. Rick Johnson and Amber Douglas provided editorial advice for revised editions. Amber also developed fidelity checklists and surveys for research studies. Listings for the Heroes Library included contributions from David Bullow, Amy Scheele, and research therapists listed.

The author is grateful to the National Child Traumatic Stress Network and Parsons Child Trauma Study Center. Research on the *Real Life Heroes* model and development of this manual was supported in part under grant number 1U70 SM54276-01 from the Substance Abuse and Mental Health Services Administration (SAMHSA), U.S. Department of Health and Human

Real Life Heroes: Practitioner's Manual
Published by The Haworth Press, Inc., 2007. All rights reserved.
doi:10.1300/5639_a

Services (HHS). The views, policies, and opinions expressed are those of the author and do not necessarily reflect those of SAMHSA or HHS.

Real Life Heroes was inspired by the courage and heroism in my own family and the families I have met in my professional practice. I am grateful to all of them, and especially for the support of my wife, Dr. Laura Kagan.

Introduction

Real Life Heroes was designed to help children with traumatic stress build the interpersonal resources needed to reintegrate painful memories and begin healing from experiences of abuse, neglect, family violence, severe illness, death, or major losses in their lives. The materials can be used as a strength-based protocol to promote a wide range of creative arts activities and guided interactions that can help a child to emotionally and cognitively process traumatic experiences. Activities are designed to rebuild or build attachments with caring committed adults and provide opportunities for caring adults to help children build skills, create safety, and overcome traumas that have impaired children's development. Ideally, activities involve caring, safe parents, but the workbook can be used to search for or foster trust with other caring adults committed to protecting, guiding, and nurturing the child *into* adulthood.

The intent of this approach is to make it safe enough for children to develop the skills and confidence needed to integrate physiological reactions, emotions, and beliefs tied to stressful experiences. The *Real Life Heroes* workbook can be used by therapists as a framework to show children that caring adults can make their world safe enough so that children can reduce their hypervigilance and threat-avoidance behaviors sufficiently to allow them to learn vital skills and gain a better understanding of how trauma shapes behavior. With each chapter, children are challenged to grow and develop skills, understanding, and beliefs that will help them cope more effectively.

By working together with therapists and caring adults, *Real Life Heroes* fosters the attachments children need in order to develop socially, emotionally, and cognitively into successful adults and to become good parents for their own children. The central challenge in this work is to find and help committed caring adults become the heroes children need in order to reestablish safety so that children can learn and develop critical skills. Workbook activities help children and caring adults to remember past events, the good and the bad times, and to create a shared story built on child, family, and cultural strengths and the courage to overcome past traumas. Caring adults become the "wise and trusted guides" that children need to become heroes in their own lives and make it possible for children to manage intense affective responses and to prevent traumatic reactions from continuing into future generations.

Rebuilding Attachments

A dual track approach is provided to foster the understanding, courage, and skills of *both* caring adults and children. Activities in the workbook provide opportunities for children and parents to bridge gaps, to communicate nonverbally and verbally, building a new or renewed sense of communication that includes self-reflection and meaning. For caring adults, activities provide opportunities to "witness" (after Herman, 1992), to demonstrate acceptance of the child's experiences, and to pass along what the adult has learned, including strengths from the child's extended family and cultural heritage that helped family members manage and overcome adversity.

Just as traumatic stress often involves breakdowns in relationships, healing is promoted by reconnecting caring adults and children: face-to-face, "brain to brain" (Siegel and Hartzell, 2003).

Real Life Heroes: Practitioner's Manual
Published by The Haworth Press, Inc., 2007. All rights reserved.
doi:10.1300/5639_b

Facial looks, tone of voice, and touch are critical to demonstrate an adult's attunement and acceptance of a child (Schore, 2003). With each page of the workbook, therapists can guide protective adults to attune to children. Shared activities can be used by caring adults to demonstrate their commitment to help disempower a child's demons and foster the child's strength and courage within a nurturing, committed relationship.

Activities provide a structure to explore and repair gaps around specific events or time periods in children's development. Repairing means acknowledging what adults have done wrong, taking responsibility for what they did, and showing children that the adult will protect them in the future. To rebuild trust, adults can share what led up to their actions and what they are going to do instead in the future. The chapters of the workbook engage children and caring adults to explore critical moments in development. Each activity provides an opportunity for caring adults to begin work on reconnecting to children and overcoming the distrust and often, the shame, fostered by events when adults acted out of control, misunderstood children, or hurt children by neglecting them or lashing out. The chapter on "Guardians and Mentors" offers tips and references for caring adults to work on understanding and, when necessary, changing their responses to children.

A Map and a Compass

Psychological assessment of a child's attachments and social, emotional, and cognitive functioning is critical to guide effective therapeutic interventions and avoid common problems in work with traumatized children. Work on attachments is most effective when based on a careful assessment of the caring and strengths of family and extended family members as well as conflicts, traumas, and safety risks in the home. This requires a careful evaluation of a child's perspective and the triggers leading to repetitive trauma behaviors. Similarly, effective work with parents and caring adults requires a careful assessment of their commitment and ability to help a child heal, adults' capacity for managing intense affective reactions, and their willingness to work on rebuilding safety, reattunement, managing their own trauma reactions, and guiding a child to maturity. Interventions work best when matched with the strengths, interests, and special talents of children and families including their ethnic and family heritage, spirituality, and ties to community resources.

When children have been placed away from their biological parents, or have been threatened with placement, it is essential to identify a primary *and* a "back-up" caring adult who would be willing to work with the child on the *Life Storybook*. Working on both reuniting and a back-up "concurrent," plan restores hope and focuses services on essential work to move children quickly out of temporary placements.

A child does not have to have a primary or back-up caring adult at the beginning of this work. The *Real Life Heroes Storybook* can be used to help identify a child's wishes for building or rebuilding attachments and thus guide service planning including: visits for the child in foster care or in-patient mental health programs, searching for caring adults, and building or rebuilding attachments.

A Developmental Model

Multiple experiences of physical or sexual abuse, domestic violence, abandonments, or other severe traumas lead to intense and repeated reactions including terror, rage, shame, avoidance, or dissociation. The developmental impact of multiple exposures to trauma often includes affective dysregulation, distrust of adults, an inability to focus and concentrate, dissociative tendencies, and breakdowns in the child's ability to succeed in school and socially with peers or adults. This pattern of responses has been described as complex trauma (Cook, Blaustein, Spinazzola, van der Kolk, et al., 2003) or developmental trauma disorder (Perry & Pollard, 1998; Pynoos & Steinberg, 2004; van der Kolk, 2005) and includes a tendency to respond to reminders of past traumas with physiological dysregulation and reenactments of previous behaviors and relationships including revictimization.

Before children are asked to work on overcoming past traumas, it is important to establish the safety, acceptance, and emotional support needed *at the developmental level* during which the children were traumatized. A fifteen-year-old who did not experience severe traumas until adolescence and is able to function socially, cognitively, and emotionally as an adolescent, may respond well to work with groups of youths. Work with such youths on skill development can be very effective, especially with a caring, dynamic, and skilled group leader utilizing a range of creative and theater arts activities (e.g., DeRosa, Pelcovitz, Kaplan, et al., 2005). In contrast, a youth who was traumatized as a preschool child, lacks a stable and safe home, and functions developmentally like a four-year-old will typically require extended individual therapy. Work with such children is often most effective involving a therapist and a caring adult working together with art, music, games, or physical skill development training to remaster traumatic incidents and learn new ways of coping. Similarly, a child who was never able to master the basic trust required for a secure attachment as a toddler will usually need to work with a therapist and a caring parent figure with repeated interactions that foster basic trust in a parent or substitute parent to care for his or her basic needs. In each case, a therapist can help a child develop more age-appropriate skills and perspectives within the newfound safety of therapeutic and family or substitute family relationships.

Relationships are crucial in this work. When traumas have impacted a child's attachments, healing means rebuilding trust that caring adults will persevere, rather than move in and out of a child's life. Even for older adolescents, it is crucial to connect each youth with someone who will actively and consistently check on them, follow up, monitor, exercise authority, and "hassle" them enough to show they care, and will continue to care over time. By focusing on both strengthening the youth and rebuilding, or building, long-term caring relationships, therapists can help children and adolescents grow beyond the developmental phase where they became traumatized.

Guiding Principles

Real Life Heroes focuses on three primary issues (Kagan, 1996) in work with children who have experienced traumatic stress:

1. Children need caring and committed adults who will care for them through good times and bad, protect and guide them now and into adulthood, and help them to integrate a life story based on mastery and hope, a life story that includes what the children saw, felt, heard, thought, and did over time.
2. Trauma processing takes place within safe relationships with therapists and caring adults who prove they are strong enough and committed enough to experience children's pain and guide children to reintegrate the fragments of their lives, to grieve losses, and to learn new behaviors. Caring adults play a critical role in trauma therapy by showing children that their experience has been heard and believed by people who care enough about them to protect them, set limits, implement safety plans, and keep the "monsters" of the past away.
3. Traumatized children and caring adults can develop skills to calm themselves, gain control over their fears and nightmares, and replace high-risk and misbehaviors with achievements that help themselves, their families, and their communities.

Building Strengths, Chapter by Chapter

The workbook provides a structured curriculum that fosters safety to engage children and caring adults in the work needed to overcome the impact of traumas. The workbook is organized into an Introduction, a Pledge, and nine chapters:

1. A Little About Me
2. Heroes
3. People in My Life
4. Good Times
5. Making Things Better
6. The ABCs of Trauma and the Hero's Challenge
7. Looking Back
8. Through the Tough Times
9. Into the Future

An "Introduction for Parents and Caring Adults" discusses effective use of this book including safety guidelines, promoting creativity, the making of heroes, how to facilitate storytelling, when to bring in a therapist, and a note for therapists. The importance of validation is stressed and the book begins with a Pledge in which helping adults promise to respect the child's perceptions, thoughts, and feelings. The Pledge marks the beginning of the adventure and a contract to strengthen or find caring, committed adults who will validate and protect the child.

Chapter 1 introduces the child to the format of the storybook. The heading at the top of the page directs the child to visualize a memory or a fantasy and then to illustrate it with a drawing or a photograph, to imagine how it would sound as a song, or, to show how it would look through movement as a dance or a movie. Therapists can use the format outlined in the *Practitioner's Manual* to engage children in creative arts activities that foster integration of experiences and enhancement of strengths. A question at the bottom of the page directs the child to write a brief note about something special in his or her picture. Questions were designed to build up a child's sense of being valued and a child's sense of competence in different situations. The completed page will typically contain both a child's visual memory and a short narrative to add additional details and the child's understanding of what was most important.

Chapter 1 provides opportunities for children to learn to recognize and express a range of feelings in a safe way. Some children find this easy and others require a great deal of practice in developing affect management skills. The manual includes guidelines for helping children learn to focus on drawing, rhythm, tonality, and movement as part of each session's structure as a means to help children work nonverbally and keep themselves within their "window of tolerance" (Siegel, 1999).

In the first few pages, children are invited to draw a little about themselves and later to share this with safe, caring adults who are helping them "write" the storybook. This process provides a means for children to test and confirm that caring adults accept that it is normal to have a wide range of feelings. This is especially important for children who have experienced separations and traumas leading them to become constricted in their feelings, beliefs, and sense of hope.

Chapter 2 helps children identify people from their families, ethnic group, community, and broader culture who have acted as heroes as a means of rekindling hope and modeling mastery over traumas. Heroes in this workbook refer to women and men, boys and girls. Children are invited to draw, act out, or write a brief story of someone in their lives who has acted like a hero.

Workbook pages help children to focus on how real people, including popular icons and fictional heroes, struggled to build strengths and overcome adversity. The importance of building strengths is accentuated and then utilized to introduce children to psychoeducational materials on trauma, building on principles from TARGET and FREEDOM (Ford & Russo, 2006, 2003), which can help children reduce feelings of shame about trauma reactions and to focus instead on skill development in recognizing and managing how they cope with trauma reminders. The manual provides specific guidelines to help children develop affect-modulation skills, calm themselves with deep-"belly" breathing, "progressive muscle relaxation," "safe place" imagery, "thought-stopping," and other affect-regulation skills.

This chapter also provides a place for children to remember how they have helped others and to envision what they could do in the future. In this way, *Real Life Heroes* helps children see how they are special within their families and communities. Helping others is an integral part of building self-esteem and shaping tomorrow's citizens and leaders. Chapter 2 emphasizes helping others as an integral part of becoming a hero.

Chapter 3 helps children to remember people who cared for them day by day, through sickness and health. Memories of being valued and of positive people are often lost or minimized when a child has experienced difficult times in his or her life. This chapter provides an opportunity to expand children's awareness of people who have helped, even in small ways, and to highlight resources in their lives including their own talents. Children can also bring in images of heroes and heroines from stories, music, movies, fantasy, and real life. Chapter 3 also provides a framework to help children to diagram the roots of their family tree, highlighting ties to family members, friends, caring adults, pets, mentors, and other sources of support.

Chapter 4 helps children to remember and build upon the strengths, skills, beliefs, and supportive relationships that helped them to enjoy "good times." Children are invited to imagine their own special holiday (after Evans, 1986), free from the constraints with which they lived. This exercise often yields important clues to a child's inner wishes and unspoken needs. Therapists can use the desires for relationships with important people identified by the child in Chapter 4 to guide work on building or rebuilding supports for the child. The intent is to help the child learn from what works in "good times" to help to master the "tough times."

Chapter 5 encourages children to look beyond magical wishes and develop the skills to make things better in their lives. This chapter includes opportunities for children to strengthen calming and self-soothing skills and develop positive beliefs in their own capacity.

In Chapter 6, children explore The ABCs of Trauma and the Hero's Challenge. This worksheet module integrates psychoeducation on trauma and CBT (cognitive behavioral therapy) exercises to help children replace dysfunctional beliefs with positive self-statements. Exercises in Chapter 6 prepare children for the difficult work ahead, transforming legacies of victimization and shaming into a self-image of surviving, coping, and growing in strength.

Chapter 7 provides a time line to record a child's moves between different locations or homes. Moves, especially for children in placement, often mean losses of relationships and lead to children feeling blamed or blaming themselves for what happened. By asking children to share what they think happened, therapists and caring adults can address dysfunctional beliefs and attributions. Learning perspectives on moves can also be used to guide services to help children find out what really happened and to provide opportunities, when necessary, for children to make up for mistakes they made that hurt other people. Information gathered in Chapter 7 can be used by therapists to help with the trauma processing and re-integration activities outlined in Chapter 8.

Children can also use Chapter 7 to develop a time line of good and bad events. Ratings of events from "worst" to "best" can help children see how forces outside their control have affected their lives and at the same time to develop a sense of time including a past, a present, and a future. This helps children develop the understanding that they don't have to remain stuck in uncomfortable positions.

After a child completes the time line, it is helpful to emphasize how we can learn from the tough times and that it is just as important to learn from the good times. Therapists can ask the child to draw a line connecting each circled number on the right side, then turn the page horizontally so the page number is on the right side. This highlights every year in the child's life when the line went up and can be used as guides to learn more from the child about what helped make things better in those years. Who helped in these special times and how did the child help himself or herself?

The time line helps to identify positive events in children's lives. By looking more closely at these important and often neglected times, caring adults can help children learn lessons about who helped them succeed, how they helped themselves, and how they and important people in their lives overcame problems. In this way, successes from the past can expand a child's sense of hope to deal with problems in the present or the future.

Before moving ahead and dealing with "Tough Times" in Chapter 8, therapists and caring adults ensure that safety plans and emotional supports are in place for the child and also for caring adults. Therapists and caring adults evaluate whether a child is ready to move on to more difficult issues by assessing the child's ability to reduce their "knots" sufficiently to manage stress without dangerous behaviors.

In Chapter 8, children are encouraged to remember and enlist the skills and resources that helped them in the past to learn from difficult times and desensitize a series of progressively more difficult "tough times." The chapter includes an opportunity for children to think about what they can do to make up for mistakes they have made. For children who have experienced a significant trauma, Chapter 8 provides an opportunity to write a story about what helped them get through "your toughest time ever" emphasizing what the children have learned and the resources utilized. After a child shares difficult situations from the past, it is helpful to engage caring adults and children in reenactments that demonstrate how the child would not be left alone and how caring adults would help a child to master what was impossible to face in the past.

Chapter 9 provides a chance for children to develop images of themselves becoming successful in the future, which highlight positive, enduring relationships and contributions of the children. This can easily lead to planning activities and educational programs to help children achieve their goals.

Completion of the Workbook

After finishing Chapters 1 through 9, children are encouraged to put their memories together into a narrative story of their life. Children can write their life stories as traditional autobiographies, using the Notes section at the end of the book, or preferably with a word processor to allow flexibility and easy revisions. The completed narrative can then be inserted into the end of the workbook.

Children develop resources and practice in expressing memories including thoughts, feelings, and actions by completing the eight chapters of the workbook. This helps traumatized children with the often difficult task of creating an integrated and strength-enhancing life story. Completing the workbook helps children desensitize reminders of painful events that in the past blocked them from being able to express a coherent and integrated narrative. "Telling the story" and reintegrating painful events becomes possible as the child grows stronger and with repeated testing and demonstration of safety plans.

Therapists and mentors working individually with children can integrate developing self-esteem with development of writing and communication skills. Writing a summary of the child's life story is facilitated by utilizing the structure of the child's time line from Chapter 7. The child can put together a summary of the most important experiences in his or her life beginning with how parents came to be together, the child's birth, and how family members have coped with good times *and* bad leading to the child's achievements. This may require "detective" work including finding safe ways to contact and interview relatives, former therapists, foster parents, and practitioners in governmental agencies who worked with the child. The narrative can emphasize how the child mastered difficult situations and developed skills with help from important people.

Children are invited to create their own title page as the final step in this book. The title should reflect how they have mastered "good times and bad." I invite children to remove the title page that came with the workbook, as well as all the guidelines for adults. Examples of titles include: "My Book About Good Times and Bad," "All About Me," "My Family and Me," "My Life from A to Z," and "How I Learned to Enjoy My Life."

By the end of the workbook, children should be able to identify people who cared about them in the past *and* the present, and who they would like to have in their lives in the future. Children should also be able to verbalize, picture, or dramatize strengths and lessons they have learned about themselves and their families. Finally, children should be able to express in words, art, music, and movement how they could manage *tough times* with the help of caring adults in the future.

Success with the workbook is fostered by:

- developing *safety* for children and their families,
- building *self-soothing skills,*
- engaging and *strengthening caring adults,* and
- helping children grow *stronger and stronger.*

Safety First

Children need to become secure enough within their primary relationships to caring adults and therapists and also within their own bodies in order to safely reexperience and reintegrate difficult memories and feelings. It is important to develop basic safety and affect regulation capacity *before* trauma processing (van der Kolk, 2003). Reexposing children to memories of victimization without developing necessary safety and affect management skills can lead to restimulation of overwhelming pain, perceptions of helplessness, and dissociative reactions (Pitman et al., 1991). Too much arousal sensitizes children and associates therapy with pain, confirming the power of the trauma. Similarly, exposing children to repeated short exposures to past traumas can strengthen trauma reactions.

Real Life Heroes utilizes a structured series of nonverbal creative arts modalities to help children feel safe enough to process past traumas and reduce trauma reactions. Activities promote self-control, creativity, substitution of fun for threat avoidance, and development of positive beliefs to counter dysfunctional thoughts that reinforce traumas. Children learn that previously unbearable memories can be managed and that thoughts and feelings can be modulated without returning to the overwhelming distress of traumatic events.

Safety and reduction of a child's threat-avoidance behaviors depends on developing and maintaining relationships with caring and committed adults. Techniques and protocols cannot replace the support children receive from caring adults and skilled therapists working step-by-step, and day by day, to help children modulate anxiety, develop skills, and develop solutions to crises that have often left children, their parents, and grandparents feeling trapped for generations. Therapy sessions can reinforce confidence through shared activities that emphasize how life is *different* now and how caring adults will protect children, even when they reexperience the smells, sounds, images, and feelings associated with past traumas.

Safety plans are a critical part of this work and need to include specific and viable plans to ensure how caring adults will work to protect the child and the people the child loves from repetitions of past violence, abuse, neglect, and loss. This begins with a careful assessment of past traumas and current dangers from the child's perspective. Healing requires validation by significant adults of the child's experiences and acceptance by caring adults of the responsibility to develop and implement step-by-step action plans for protection of children and family members.

Caring adults often need to build skills for self-soothing, affect management, safe relationships, parenting, and conflict management. Parents and other adults facilitate healing by demonstrating to children that *they* can handle reminders of traumatic events without losing control of their own affective responses.

Affect management skills can be fostered through support groups, classes on parenting, anger management, and prevention of domestic violence, *and* work in *individualized* therapy to develop and implement *personal* safety plans. Completing a class helps provide vital information, but is rarely sufficient to effect change. Children, parents, and authorities need to share, understand, and experience over time that safety and relapse-prevention plans have been implemented.

Children cannot simply begin trusting a Mother or Father who was not able, or was unwilling to stop neglect or violence. Trust is impossible when parents remain locked in denial of how their children were harmed, or worse, continue to threaten children. If children were hurt by physical or sexual abuse and coerced into keeping secrets, they very likely will never be able to fully trust that parent again and may also never be able to completely rely on a nonabusive parent who failed to keep them safe. Non-family protectors, orders of protection, alarm systems, and guard dogs may be necessary for these children to feel safe enough to grow.

A parent or caring adult will typically need to prove that the child is safe for at least the same amount of time that the abuse and neglect was allowed to continue. So, if parents were too overwhelmed to protect a child for a year, it will usually take another year of validation and testing to rebuild the trust that was lost. Families can celebrate passing the anniversary dates of past traumas as a way to demonstrate how much they have changed and how children no longer have to be afraid.

In the interim, other caring adults need to be involved in a child's life and show the child that they will watch for signs of the violence or neglect cycle starting again and take action if this happens. Bringing in strong caring adults becomes a key part of safety plans for children to reunite with parents and families where neglect or violence took place.

Self-Soothing Skills

Chapter 1's exercises provide a starting point for developing and practicing self-soothing and self-monitoring skills. Children need to utilize self-soothing skills in order to replace the hyperarousal, irritability, and inability to relax that is often part of complex trauma reactions. For children with high levels of anxiety, it is important to find ways to reassure them, to help them to relax, and to strengthen their sense of security *before* completing Chapter 8. The objective is to help a child to feel calm enough to be able to think and try out different ways to manage previously stressful situations.

Developing "safe place" imagery is very helpful. Children should be able to bring up relaxing images of a place and a time when they felt safe. This can be practiced with tapping, eye movements, alternating sounds (Shapiro, 2001), repeated soft chords, or other simple repetitive and soothing aids. Patterned repetitive stimulation may "trick" or calm a trauma-activated brainstem into allowing the child to learn new ways to perceive and cope with traumatic events (see, e.g., Shapiro, 2001, and Tinker & Wilson, 1999, for information on use of EMDR). Healing rituals, such as prayer alongside a comforting adult, drumming, chanting, dance, or singing hymns and reassuring tunes may also be very helpful.

Children can be guided in developing self-soothing skills with exercises in deep muscle relaxation, visual imagery, and meditation (Munson & Riskin, 1995; Cohen, Mannarino, & Deblinger, 2003; Cohen et al., 2006). For children who have difficulty managing frustrations and anger, exercises in anger management may be very useful (Eggert, 1994; Whitehouse & Pudney, 1996). Similarly, children with difficulties focusing attention may benefit from workbooks that provide guidance around slowing down and sustaining attention (Nadeau & Dixon, 1997).

Strengthening Caring Adults

Parents and caring adults confront a paradox in their efforts to rescue traumatized children. The children themselves often resist caring adults' efforts to change their lives and act as "threshold guardians" (Campbell, 1968). It often appears safer for children to remain immersed in repeated crises than to risk changes and the pain of reexperiencing another breakdown of trust or attachment. Caring adults may face a fiercely resistant child guarding the door to healing, reunification, or adoption.

Underneath the defiance and resistance of a traumatized child, caring adults can find the hurt child. Therapists can help caring adults persevere with the understanding that a child's "problem behaviors" often mark his or her unspoken terror and can light a path to both a child's pain and solutions (Kagan, 2003). Children's behaviors can guide therapists and caring adults to core dilemmas, often the traumas that led to the breakdowns of trust and attachments. Therapists can help caring adults understand how traumas have led to children's behaviors and have been reinforced as survival mechanisms. Rather than focusing on demands for children to stop problem behaviors, caring adults can demonstrate to children that their old behaviors are not needed anymore, that caring adults will not respond with the abuse, neglect, rejections, or abandonment that traumatized children have often come to expect, and that together, caring adults and children can develop and new ways of coping with reminders of past traumas.

Real Life Heroes challenges children to cross the "threshold" into a different world, a life in which parents (biological, kinship, or adoptive) and other caring adults dare to face children's worst nightmares. This may begin with promises or legal papers, but these mean little to a traumatized child. Trust requires confronting and passing the tests of fire from a child's past.

The secrets of success for caring adults, just as in mythic stories, revolve around learning from each challenge and from the "threshold guardians" (Campbell, 1968). Hurt and hurting children provide clues to solutions. Claiming and guiding children helps them succeed. Blaming, labeling, and rejection foster obstacles and turmoil.

Therapists can serve as mentors to help caring adults and children learn from provocative behaviors and to remain focused on helping caring adults become heroes for their children. Therapists can help parents to understand and then detach themselves from a children's behaviors, building on the caring side of family members, and empowering parents with skills, support, and a little magic in the eyes of their children. Symbolically, *Real Life Heroes* can help to demystify children and remystify and empower caring adults.

Therapists can guide caring adults to calm themselves, to step back, to listen with their hearts, to watch for patterns of behavior, and to welcome a child's challenges as clues to discover a child's past. Troubling children often reenact interactions stemming from past traumas. This gives returning or adoptive parents the opportunity to enter their children's "real" world, and become "real" parents by overcoming their worst nightmares. For caring adults and therapists, this means strengthening themselves with understanding, skills, and support so that they can feel a child's pain and develop an understanding of the perceptions, beliefs, and feelings of the child's world, no matter how frightening or how close a child's terrors may be to the adult's own experiences.

By accepting the challenge behind each behavior, therapists and caring adults open up solutions to a child's fears, which typically revolve around critical traumas in their past and often, very real experiences of abandonment and violence. Therapists can use behavioral messages as keys to the doors that act as barriers, separating the hurting child from the wounded child within. Crises can be utilized as the "calls to adventure" (Campbell, 1968) by which children *test* the reality of parents' commitment and the promises of a better life in their new world.

Research and Evaluation Studies

Therapists have consistently reported positive results during eight years of case studies with children with complex PTSD involved in home-based or clinic-based family counseling and with children who have been living in foster families and residential treatment centers due to dangerous behaviors and repeated experiences of physical or sexual abuse, and neglect. A pilot research study (Kagan, Douglas, Hornik & Kratz, in press) was conducted to evaluate the effectiveness of this model with forty-one children and adolescents at Parsons Child and Family Center, a community practice site of the National Child Traumatic Stress Network. Data from the Parsons study were utilized to assess changes from enrollment and at four, eight, and twelve months of treatment. Therapists reported that the model helped them to engage children who had experienced neglect, abandonment, physical and sexual abuse, domestic violence, multiple losses, and separations including histories of placements away from families of origin. The curriculum helped therapists persevere with application of cognitive behavioral therapy components over time as noted on chapter checklists and in informal feedback sessions.

At four months, children (N = 36) demonstrated reductions (p<.05) in:

- Trauma symptoms on child self-reports evaluated with the Trauma Symptom Checklist for Children, TSCC (Briere, 1996)
- Problem behaviors reported by primary caretakers on the Conners Behavior Rating Scale—Parent-Long Version (Conners, 1997)

At the end of the twelve-month study period (N = 25), results included:

- Reduced trauma symptoms reported by the adult caregiver on the PROPS (Greenwald & Rubin, 1999a,b) in relation to the number of *Real Life Heroes* chapters completed (p<.001)
- Increased security/attachment over time reported by the child (p<.05) on the Security Scale (Kerns, Klepac & Cole, 1996)

The pilot study did not include a control group and does not establish the efficacy of this model. However, results supported the model's effectiveness to reduce symptoms of traumatic stress and increase children's security with primary caregivers.

Stronger and Stronger

Chapter by chapter, children build stronger identities. Chapter 20 includes a chart that can be copied and used to help reinforce a child's progress in completing the workbook. At the end of Chapter 8, children can compare their drawings of themselves as heroes with their image of themselves from a "tough time" in the past. Therapists can help children visualize how they have grown while their problems stayed the same size (Rojano, 1998) or shrank in power.

Therapists can adapt the workbook to individual children by selecting the most relevant pages. The most important activities are highlighted in italics; these pages have also been found to be especially useful in assessments of critical factors for work on rebuilding attachments, grieving losses, and healing. By combining the structured approach of the life storybook with more open-ended art, music, dance, or other modalities, therapists can help children to recover important connections and skills that may have been lost after traumas and to develop solutions beyond the constraints of verbal expression.

The workbook can be used very much like a guide or map for the journey ahead. Through activities and collaborative work, children can build on strengths and resources to rewrite their life story. In this way, life story work can be used not just to tell a child's story, but to rebuild a story of people who cared and will care for a child through his or her lifetime. The heroes in the child's life story are the real people who define what it means for a child to belong to a family and a community, people with the courage to help transform a hurt and hurting child into a hero for the future.

Manual Organization

The manual provides detailed guidelines for therapists and is organized, chapter by chapter:

- Objectives
- Overview
- Step by Step (key points and sequence)
- Pitfalls (problems that can undermine therapy)
- Troubleshooting (challenges and solutions)
- Checkpoints (essential elements)

A Session Summary/Progress Note is provided in Chapter 21. It includes an easy-to-complete check-off format that targets critical issues, safety plans, trauma triggers, and constructive versus dysfunctional beliefs. A bookmark is provided in Chapter 22 to highlight key components and sequences for sessions. The bookmark also serves as a reminder to children of the session structure. A guide to recommended materials/supplies is included at the beginning of the manual.

Rebuilding Attachments with Traumatized Children: Healing from Losses, Violence, Abuse, and Neglect (Kagan, 2004) includes comprehensive discussion of trauma and attachment theory, research, and detailed guidelines for therapeutic interventions including tools for assessment and service planning, engaging parents and guardians, permanency work, and activities to promote secure attachments. *Rebuilding Attachments* includes practical tools for helping children and caring adults overcome adversity and transform themselves from victims to heroes in their own lives.

For advocacy, recruitment, and trauma training in foster care, adoption, and child and family services, please see *Wounded Angels: Lessons of Courage from Children in Crisis* (Kagan, 2003). *Wounded Angels* includes stories of how traumatized children challenge therapists, parents, teachers, and policymakers to work together to overcome the power of terror and how we can utilize children's behaviors to engage caring adults, develop effective services to overcome core dilemmas of families in crisis, and renew hope for healing after chronic and severe traumas.

PART I:
FIRST STEPS—
PREPARING FOR THE JOURNEY

Materials and Supplies

The following list suggests inexpensive materials that can be utilized to make therapy sessions a special time and place where each child can become free to explore, create, and develop skills. Materials have also been found to be very conducive to fostering attunement activities involving caring adults and children.

For Children

- Deluxe sets of washable markers and colored pencils stored in an attractive case, ideally including both large and fine-pointed markers and at least a dozen colors including different skin shades.
- Xylophone (glockenspiel) with four mallets with two-octave scale; ideally, one for child and one for therapist or caring adult. (These can be found on many Web sites.)
- Peacock feathers, sterilized, stem-dyed tail with full eyes, thirty-five to forty inches long, shed naturally by peacocks.
- Rhythm instruments: homemade drum, xylophone, etc.
- Craft materials: beads, clay, ribbons, children's scissors.
- Collage materials: teen and sports magazines appropriate for often oversexualized youths.
- Copies of *Real Life Heroes: A Life Storybook for Children,* 2007 edition.
- Tape recorder for recording children's music and "interviews."
- Mirror (large enough to capture the child's upper body, or ideally the child's whole body, mirror can be wall mounted).
- Feelings charts: see, e.g., *Childswork/Childsplay* (GuidanceChannel.com).
- Reference materials: books, movies, and CDs about heroes matched to each child's ethnic background, sex, age, and reading level (see Chapter 16).
- If possible: camera or video camera, preferably digital or Polaroid, for viewing and printing images and enactments in each session.
- Case or bag to carry supplies for home and community-based work.

Real Life Heroes: Practitioner's Manual
Published by The Haworth Press, Inc., 2007. All rights reserved.
doi:10.1300/5639_01

For Caring Adults

- Copies of the *Real Life Heroes Life Storybook* for caring adults.
- Resources for Caring Adults (see Chapter 15); see especially: *Wounded Angels: Lessons from Children in Crisis* (Child Welfare League of America) and *Parenting from the Inside Out* (Tarcher/Putnam).
- Musical instruments, art tools, camera, mirror, etc., from children's list.

A Map and a Compass:
Trauma and Attachment-Centered
Service Planning

Objectives

- Promote shared understanding of a developmental, strength-based trauma and attachment-centered model of intervention.
- Engage parents, guardians, foster parents, child-care workers, teachers, governmental authorities, and other therapists to utilize a developmental, trauma and attachment-centered framework to develop service plans and manage behavior problems.

Overview

Before embarking on the journey of therapy with children and families who have experienced traumatic stress, it is important to have a map and a compass. For *Real Life Heroes* (RLH), the map is a strength-based attachment and trauma-centered assessment of children and families. The compass is a service planning tool that keeps therapists and caring adults focused on overcoming the core issues that have often constricted child and family development. The RLH assessment and service plan reframes child and adult interactive behaviors as clues to children's developmental functioning, resources, traumatic stress reactions, and how we can use this understanding to overcome obstacles, reduce dangerous behaviors, and promote development.

In child and family services, assessment often has to be rapid with an understanding that this will be an ongoing process over the course of therapy and tied at every step to engagement and interventions. Children and primary caretakers often test quickly to see if professionals will repeat past problems, participate in reenactments of crisis cycles, or leave them feeling disrespected, shamed, labeled, neglected, rejected, or abandoned.

Therapists can use a developmentally based trauma and attachment assessment guide to engage children and family members and to develop initial contracts, thus increasing hope that *this* therapeutic "journey" will be *different,* or at least, worth trying (even if a child or parent is court-ordered to participate). Focusing on attachments, traumas, and strengths helps ensure family members that they will be treated with respect at every step of the journey. Therapists can serve as guides, but Moms and Dads, grandparents, foster/adoptive parents, and child-care workers must carry on after the session, 24-7, week after week. Service planning has to be geared to their strengths and needs.

Children who have experienced severe and repeated traumas can also be expected to test caring adults, and especially whenever their current sense of balance, however precarious, is threatened. Change is hard and children who demonstrate high-risk behaviors have often learned that change is dangerous. Many children believe that it is safer to remain suspended, placed, hospitalized, or incarcerated than to face the possibility of a secret being exposed or a family member going to jail, going "crazy," or committing suicide. Accordingly, children often pull or provoke

Real Life Heroes: Practitioner's Manual
Published by The Haworth Press, Inc., 2007. All rights reserved.
doi:10.1300/5639_02

therapists and caring adults to reenact past rejections, neglect, or abandonments. Rebuilding trust and attachments means working in person, one to one, using our sensitivity and understanding, and moving beyond behaviors that may function like storms or fog that can put everyone off course.

Testing and contracting begin from the first contacts with a child and other family members. For that reason, a focused assessment of trauma and service planning give family members a strong message that this intervention will be *different*. By using an understanding of a child's development and traumatic reaction patterns as a compass, therapists can help chart a course so that caring adults stay on course and avoid reenactments of past traumas.

Step by Step

Use of the RLH workbook with traumatized children should include careful assessments focused on attachments and traumas including individual evaluations of the child alone and involving significant family members.

Utilize the "Five-Step Brief Assessment and Service Planning" guide in Chapter 17 as a starting point for developmental, trauma, and attachment assessments. This guide is also useful along the journey to keep work focused on attachment and trauma issues, especially when interactive behavior problems stymie progress. A checklist and the outline can be copied for processing referrals, contracting sessions, and review conferences.

As soon as possible, begin the Attachment Ecogram, the Attachment and Trauma Assessment and Service Planning worksheets, and the interview guide for Important People included in Chapters 17 and 18. The Attachment Ecogram (Kagan, 2004b) includes a time line and diagram of family-community relationships. The Attachment Trauma worksheets incorporate critical components of trauma and attachment reactions and checklists for trauma and attachment interventions.

Use of the Trauma Symptom Checklist for Children (Briere, 1996), the UCLA PTSD Reaction Index for DSM-IV (Pynoos, Rodriquez, Steinberg, Stuber & Frederick, 1998), the Trauma Symptom Checklist for Young Children (Briere, 1996), the Security Scale (Kerns, Klepac & Cole, 1996), the Roberts Apperception Test (Roberts, 1986), and Projective Storytelling Cards (Casebeer Art Productions, 1989) are recommended as part of assessments. Use of these instruments demonstrates to children and parents that therapists are able to talk about difficult issues, e.g., sexual abuse and can often open discussion of otherwise unspoken traumas. Behavior rating scales such as the Conners Parent Rating Scale, Long version (Conners, 1997) or Child Behavior Checklist (Achenbach & Rescoria (2000a, b) are useful for differentiating anxiety reactions from ADHD and disruptive behavior problems.

Assessments should include evaluation for dissociation and life-threatening behaviors. *Real Life Heroes* is not recommended for youths who are actively suicidal or engaging in life-threatening behaviors. Formal inventories of dissociation may be necessary to assess a child's stability and differentiate dissociation from drug-induced behaviors. Symptoms of dissociation that warrant caution and safety measures include:

• Mumbled, garbled verbalizations
• Repetitive movements
• Lack of awareness of time or place
• Lack of awareness of the therapist's identity or of self
• Trancelike movements or visual fixations
• Sudden changes in movement that don't fit with the child's stories
• Inability to remember if they really did something or just imagined doing it
• Not being able to remember actions observed by others

- Finding themselves in a place and not knowing how they got there
- Inability to feel parts of their body
- Hearing voices or seeing things that weren't really there

Pitfalls

- Children or parents believe they are given diagnoses that block change.
- Therapists and caring adults reenact the child's traumas.
- Therapists accept beliefs at referral that no one cares, no one is available, and only professionals can manage the problems presented.

Troubleshooting

If . . .	Then . . .
Contracts require acceptance of all referrals on a **No Reject, No Eject basis,**	Use trauma and attachment assessments to introduce phase-based work as part of initial contract sessions, demonstrating through assessments that parents and other caring adults choosing to work will be treated with respect for individual, family, and cultural strengths and values, while at the same time using sessions to overcome very real traumas and on-going safety issues. That means including trauma, attachment, and developmental assessments as part of the work.
Parents or other family members **balk at sharing, feeling forced to participate,**	Emphasize from the start that therapists need family members' help to help their child. Look for and accentuate signs of caring and pain shared by children and adults. Utilize engaging messages including affirmation of guardian rights to work with other therapists and agencies and openness about purpose of sessions. Invite children and parents to share their expectations for the assessment and share how therapists ask 'nosey' questions and will count on family members to stop them if this becomes too sensitive (Kagan & Schlosberg, 1989). For detailed guidelines for engaging and assessing families referred after abuse and neglect, see Families in Perpetual Crisis (Kagan & Schlosberg, 1989).

Checkpoints

_____ Therapist identifies current and potential caring adults who can validate, protect, and guide child

_____ Therapist completes the Brief Guides to Assessment and Service Planning and starts an Attachment Ecogram (Chapter 17)

Guardians and Mentors:
Finding and Strengthening Caring Adults

Objectives

Engage, or if necessary, begin search for, at least two, and optimally, three or more, caring adults committed to guiding child to maturity.

Assist caring adults to:

- Develop an understanding of how trauma impacts a child's neural development and behaviors and conversely how attachments can help a child learn to overcome past traumas.
- Develop and implement viable safety plans that demonstrate to child that the parent, along with other caring adults, will work to protect the child from repetitions of past traumas.
- Demonstrate that they can manage stressors and reminders linked to child's and parents' past traumas without losing control or ability to keep family members safe.
- Demonstrate that they can listen and validate a child's perspective.
- Write their own life story to be shared with child after Safety Steps have been accomplished.

Overview

Real Life Heroes engages and mobilizes parents, or if necessary, substitute caretakers, to become the guardians and mentors for the journey ahead. The intent is to find at least two, and optimally three or more, caring adults who will validate, support, and guide each child with a commitment to raising the child to maturity. That way, if the child loses his or her primary caring adult, e.g., to illness or disability, the child will still be able to count on at least one other adult to keep the child safe. This is similar to having a guardian listed in a will, or a godparent in many cultures, and a critical step in safety planning for children who have learned that they could lose their primary caretakers to substance abuse, life-threatening illnesses, family violence, incarceration, natural disasters, wars, or community violence.

When parents are unable or unwilling to care for children, the workbook can be used as an aid to search for and engage other caring adults, e.g., grandparents, aunts, uncles, older siblings, mentors, clergy. However, even when parents and grandparents have abandoned or harmed children, it is important for children to learn about strengths from their families' heritage and culture.

Family members may present initially as resistant to counseling or focused on blaming one or more children as the primary problems in the family. Parents often feel unfairly blamed, or shamed, when their children are harmed, especially if children have been abused or neglected or experienced domestic violence. Family members often misunderstand how children experience traumatic events in a different and often much more distressing manner than adults. For instance, a mother knocked to the floor and cursed by a father or boyfriend may pick herself up

Real Life Heroes: Practitioner's Manual
Published by The Haworth Press, Inc., 2007. All rights reserved.
doi:10.1300/5639_03

and go back to what she was doing. Children, on the other hand, may see the blood on her cheek as much more of a "life or death" crisis. If the parent is unable to comfort and reassure the child, the child may become even more distressed. Later, the child may act out what happened, for instance, hitting and knocking down a younger sibling, which leads the mother, in this example, to scream and punish the child, and possibly causing the child to feel even more detached and distressed.

Children's behavioral manifestations of trauma may be reinforced when acting out. Unspoken problems gives children a sense of control and refocuses family members away from traumatic events and recurrent dangers. By focusing on how trauma works neurologically, behaviorally, and in families over time, therapists can help children's natural caretakers move away from shame over what they did or failed to do, and instead work on helping children and families heal.

Shame and blame are also reduced when therapists stress that caring adults are essential to protect, provide, and guide children (James, 1989, 1994). This begins with how family members are welcomed into service planning and decision making. Therapists can also assist by respecting and responding to essential needs of families, e.g., safe housing, safe schools, and after-school supervision, which must be met before children and parents can address past traumas.

A comprehensive assessment is critical for this work and needs to address safety for children and caring adults, attachments, developmental levels, affect regulation, ability to "tell the story" of past traumas, trauma processing, and relationships with peers and community. With a trauma- and attachment-based assessment (see "A Map and a Compass"), therapists can often engage caring adults by evaluating and then highlighting how the behaviors and pain the therapist sees in traumatized children is shared by family members and other caring adults who love the child. When children feel that their bodies, their hearts or their souls are broken, caring adults also often feel that their hearts or souls are broken (Madanes, 1990).

Caring adults can empower themselves with an understanding of how trauma works and show children that by working together, committed adults, therapists, and children can change their lives. Therapists and caring adults can also use an understanding of trauma to frame interventions that can help to rebuild trust at the developmental level where a child's attachments broke down. To do this, caring adults need to show children that they are able to listen and learn from children, to watch children's behaviors for clues to fears and strengths, to listen to children's voices, and to respect children's perspectives. By doing this, caring adults make the *Pledge* come true.

Caring adults benefit from learning and practicing the stress-reduction skills in the workbook's Chapters 1 and 2: deep belly breathing, safe place imagery, thought stopping, progressive muscle relaxation, "SOS" (Ford & Russo, 2006), as well as reprocessing and replacing beliefs that increase shame and stress (workbook Chapter Six). Encourage adults, as well as children, to understand how thoughts come and go (Cohen, Mannarino & Deblinger, 2003) and allow them to observe this process. By focusing on breathing and safe imagery, adults can learn to calm themselves and break out of longstanding patterns of reactivity, thus demonstrating to children that they can remain in control, even when children provoke them with reminders of past traumas. Taking control is also enhanced with exercises in which the adult purposely brings to mind an upsetting event (Cohen, et al, 2003) before utilizing thought-stopping and relaxation techniques.

Caring adults can help children process traumas by modeling how it is healthy to share both good and bad memories without shame or embarrassment. Caring adults lead the way for traumatized children by working on their own life stories (Mullin, 2000) at the same time, or just ahead of the children. When significant adults work on their own life stories, children see that these adults are really not afraid of the monsters or demons of the past, and that life story work is valued. Caring adults can also use life story work to demonstrate to children what they have learned and how they are changing all of their lives, building on individual, family, and cultural strengths to protect children and strengthen families.

Parents or guardians may need to develop effective behavior-management skills and to break out of cycles of behavior with children characterized by yelling, criticism, and negative attention, neglect, or a lack of guidance. Learning to ignore unwanted behaviors and to notice and accentuate positives is an essential skill in itself. Use of discipline that promotes learning and avoids reinforcement of negative behavior is also important. Teaching parents to utilize praise, actively ignoring negative behavior, and time outs (one minute per chronological year of age) have been found to be very helpful (Cohen et al., 2003). The need for guidance to develop safety and the importance of healthy expectations is also important for overcoming trauma. For example, to paraphrase Lucy Berliner (2004), even a traumatized child needs to "take out the garbage."

Step by Step

Demonstrate to parents and guardians accompanying children to therapy sessions that "we need you to help your child." Involve potential caring adults including grandparents, godparents, mentors, and clergy, whenever possible. In family work with complex PTSD and chaotic, disorganized attachments to primary caretakers, it is important to bring in additional caring adults by the third or fourth session so that work does not become mired for months and years on trying to help a child rebuild an attachment to just one parent who the child may never have been able to trust.

Provide psychoeducation, and where possible, books such as *Parenting from the Inside Out* (Siegel & Hartzell, 2003) and *Wounded Angels: Lessons from Children in Crisis* (Kagan, 2003). These books discuss how trauma including abuse, neglect, and family violence shapes neural development and how we can use children's behavior as clues to unresolved traumas and pathways to healing. Help caring adults understand the following:

- The impact of past traumas on their child's neurological functioning and behaviors including development of adaptive behaviors including: defensive avoidance, dissociation, hypervigilance, impulsive responses, and reenactments.
- How experiences of abuse and neglect split a child between craving attachment and defending against further violence.
- How behavior problems, reflect trauma reactions reinforced over time including tendencies to react to reminders of traumas by fighting, fleeing, or freezing and patterns of oppositional and defiant behavior.
- The critical role of parents and caring adults and the power of attachments help a child's neural development and recovery from traumas.
- How caring adults can help children to:
  — identify their feelings,
  — reach out for help from safe adults,
  — calm themselves, and
  — utilize adaptive behaviors to help themselves and others.
- How caring adults can help children desensitize reactions to trauma reminders by modeling self-care and calming.
- How caring adults can help children identify their beliefs and utilize more adaptive thinking to change behavior.
- How support by caring adults for life story work can identify resources and traumatic events, desensitize known (and unknown) trauma reminders, and reshape behavior.

- The importance of understanding oneself in order to help one's child. If possible, encourage caring adults to complete "Questions for Parental Self-Reflection" exercise from *Parenting from the Inside Out* (Siegel & Hartzell, 2003, pp. 133-134).
- Recommend readings from "Resources for Caring Adults" (Chapter 15) and encourage caring adults to foster reading every day with children from Heroes Library (Chapter 16). Encourage also sharing stories with children and homework exercises such as creating a video story of a child's day or a story of a visit back to where the child first lived as a baby.
- A summary of *Real Life Heroes* is provided in Chapter 14 and may be useful as an outline to share with collateral professionals or other caring adults helping a child and interested in the model.
- Assist caring adults to strengthen their own lives and help their children by developing and demonstrating over time:
  — Supportive connections with family members, friends, and community groups.
  — Self-soothing skills including: deep belly breathing, safe place imagery, thought stopping, and progressive muscle relaxation.
  — Understanding of adults' triggers and reactions.
  — Replacement of dysfunctional beliefs about trauma reactions.
  — Ability to regulate reactions to specific triggers for adult and child.
  — Fun activities with child and supportive family members and friends.

Encourage caring adults to write their own stories as a powerful means of helping their children succeed, to overcome often multigenerational traumas, and to stay a step ahead of their children. To do this, caring adults should go through each chapter of the workbook and respond to workbook pages using modalities they prefer. Adults can utilize the workbook as an outline and respond with narrative, art, music, video clips, photographs with attached narratives, audio interviews, or other means that build on their own strengths and talents. Writing life stories can be presented as a means for caring adults to pass along lessons they have learned and values they want to transmit as part of their legacy to children.

Emphasize the importance of caring adults understanding how traumatic stress affects bodily reactions and behaviors. Discuss meaning of normal stress versus traumatic stress using Chapter 23 of this manual, including key concepts:

- Traumatic stress can be described as an alarm that can't be turned off (Ford & Russo, 2006) coupled with overwhelming feelings, confused thinking, agitation, and often, impulsive behaviors. With severe, life-threatening trauma, a child (or adult) may feel helpless. The ensuing panic cuts off verbal reasoning. Words, thoughts, and feelings cannot be integrated. The child may survive the event but continue to act "as if" the danger is still present. For instance, a child who witnesses his or her parents cursing, then fighting, one parent storming out the door, and the other left bleeding, may become ultrasensitive to angry voices at school. This is especially likely if the child believes the violence has not really ended and may happen again today, tonight, or another day. If the child senses a teacher or peers getting angry or threatening, the child may freeze, hide, run away, or become agitated and aggressive. These behaviors make no sense without a contextual understanding of how the child remains in an unresolved state of alarm.
- Children can develop traumatic stress reactions after severe neglect, abuse, injuries, severe illnesses, deaths of family members or friends, domestic violence, or the breakdown of attachments. Violence is especially devastating when preschool children experience bodily harm, including the sight of blood on themselves or someone they love. The horror of witnessing an assault, sexual abuse, or parents fighting becomes too much to bear, especially for very young children. Children who have experienced violence in their homes or com-

munities may draw pictures of their homes with broken windows, knife-shaped objects, or large, sharply pointed fingers on adults' hands. Witnessing the beatings of parents or siblings shatters a child's sense of security and often leads to dysregulated behaviors, which in turn, stress parents, teachers, and families who may be struggling with family or community violence.

- Severe traumatic stress and PTSD typically result from experiences in which children perceive that they, or people they love, are threatened with severe harm (or death) and they cannot escape or help the people in danger. This often leads to survival responses including adrenaline rushes; speeding up; intense anxiety; exhaustion; lack of ability to think, plan, or reason; feelings of being overwhelmed; intrusive memories; outbursts; and impulsive, often risky behaviors. PTSD is primarily a disorder of arousal, the "alarm bells that can't be turned off" (Ford & Russo, 2006). If the experience is never reintegrated, and especially when threatening experiences are repeated, these survival responses can become habitual behaviors which, in turn, interfere with a child's development of cognitive, social, and emotional skills or attempts to rebuild relationships and attachments. Traumatic stress interferes with a child's development (van der Kolk, 2005).

- The good news for caring adults and children is that a great deal has been learned about what helps children (and adults) to overcome traumas. Most evidence-supported models have common elements:
  — safety planning for children, families, and practitioners;
  — trauma psychoeducation;
  — developing affect regulation and self-control skills;
  — reintegration of traumatic experiences;
  — identification of triggers that lead to trauma reactions and safety planning for each; and
  — reintegration into family, community, school, and work including helping others.

- In addition, effective programs are strength-based, culturally sensitive, interdisciplinary, and empowering for children, caring adults, practitioners, and communities. For children who have experienced multiple and severe traumas, including almost all children in placement or at high risk of placement, effective programs also need to rebuild (or build) attachments and address developmental levels.

Real Life Heroes incorporates these components in a chapter-by-chapter skill-building curriculum. Caring adults play a critical role in this process beginning with developing their own understanding of how trauma works, safety planning, and helping children develop the trust and skills to overcome the nightmares in their lives. In this process, children can change how they view themselves and their families, developing a stronger sense of themselves, their families, and their cultural heritage.

The *Real Life Heroes* Pilot Study (Kagan et al., in press) included Julian Ford's conceptualization of FREEDOM versus being TRAPPED (Ford & Russo, 2006) as one tool to engage and challenge children to move beyond traumatic stress responses and overcome the nightmares and fears that get in their way, preventing them (or adults) from accomplishing what is most important. (See www.ptsdfreedom.org for detailed guidelines on use of TARGET materials developed by Julian Ford.) FREEDOM emphasizes skill development including: Focus, Recognition of triggers, identifying Emotions, Evaluating thoughts and beliefs, Defining goals, Options, and Making the world better. Within this model, parents can learn how to recognize their own trauma reactions, and develop skills, step-by-step, to calm themselves and then be able to help their children learn with practice to "SOS": "Slow down, Orient yourself, Self Check." These skills are introduced in workbook Chapter 2 as part of Traumatic Stress and the Hero's Challenge (Part I) and then reintegrated in a cognitive behavioral exercise as part of workbook Chapter 6, The ABCs of Trauma and the Hero's Challenge (Part II).

For additional references and information on traumatic stress, see Chapter 2 of Kagan, 2004b; Cook et al., 2003; Siegel, 1999; Siegel & Hartzell, 2003; and van der Kolk, 2005. *Wounded Angels: Lessons from Children in Crisis* (Kagan, 2003) is helpful for adults interested in learning how children show the traumas they have experienced.

Discuss and practice how to share parent's life story with child:

- How to keep child safe.
- How to monitor child's reactions.
- How to talk about painful events to child, stressing strengths and resilience, and presenting what happened in a way child can manage at the child's developmental age level.

Help parents and guardians develop effective skills to manage their children's behaviors without rekindling fears of neglect, abandonment, or abuse experienced by child. See Cohen et al. (2003), Ford and St. Juste (2006), Kagan (2004a), and Kolko and Swenson (2002) for detailed guides on developing skills for self-control and management of children's "testing" and provocative behavior without overreacting. Working with caring adults as partners in the quest provides a framework to foster the capacity and skills to:

- step back,
- observe children's behavior without reacting,
- discover what leads up to problems (triggers),
- consider how behavior fits with past traumas,
- remind oneself that child is responding to alarm bells going off based on past experiences,
- if necessary, calm down with "SOS" (Ford & Russo, 2006, 2003), turn down the alarm, refocus attention, and make choices to succeed,
- increase reinforcement and time for skill building, catching children doing good things, and
- minimize reinforcement including negative attention to misbehaviors.

Promote the use of natural and logical consequences and an understanding of discipline as a teaching tool rather than a punishment. For attachment-impaired children, discipline needs to be centered on rebuilding trust and avoiding reexperiences of rejection, detachment, and abandonment. Caring adults need to stay in charge, modeling self-control. Attachment-impaired children need to be kept in sight. Please see *Rebuilding Attachments with Traumatized Children* (Kagan, 2004b, Chapters 6 and 7) and *Facilitating Developmental Attachment* (Hughes, 1997) for detailed guides to reparative parenting.

Since children with traumatic stress and attachment problems often feel out of control, it is very important that parents, teachers, and therapists provide opportunities for children to learn control. Caring adults can do this while still remaining in charge and maintaining safety by setting rules and enforcing limits that give children limited choices they can manage at their developmental level. Giving children two choices helps avoid power struggles and avoids triggering children by making them once again feel out of control, helpless, and on the way to more trauma (Blaustein, 2006). For instance, a child can be given a choice to do his or her math assignment right after school or right after dinner, or to pick up the toys in his or her room before or right after lunch. For a child who is violating rules, tell the child he or she can: (1) sit on the time-out chair in sight of the parent quietly (reading, writing, drawing, etc.) for five to ten minutes (i.e., one minute for each year), or the child can sit and be as loud as he or she wants for twice as long, e.g., ten to twenty minutes (after Hughes, 1997).

Parents or youths may present severe and chronic behavior problems from the first contact session with therapists or soon after entry into a foster family or group care placement. To avoid being caught up in reenactments of the youth's traumas, please see the brief guide to Developmentally Focused Behavior Management (see Exhibit I.1). Avoiding reenactments and promoting trust should be key elements of discipline. These five-step reminder guidelines were designed to help caring adults and therapists step back, use their nonverbal awareness of their own reactions, reflect on what has triggered the child's behavior, understand how the child's past experiences have shaped his or her behaviors, and then respond with as few words as possible to help the child learn more adaptive coping skills.

Help caring adults recognize how everyone can become stressed and make mistakes, e.g., modeling dysregulation or anger, when we want to teach self-control. Children may back away in fear. It's important to repair the disconnection. We can also use our mistakes as opportunities to model how to apologize and make up for ways we may have hurt others. This begins with acknowledgement, taking responsibility for what we did, and reflecting on what led to it, e.g., "I was worried that you'd get hurt. I didn't listen to you. I should have stopped, taken a break, and listened. I'm sorry I snapped at you." Then, we can outline what we will do different next time, and, even better, practice it.

Promote storytelling, e.g., sharing an experience together; reviewing each day with young children before bed, putting words on what happened including nonverbal emotional reactions; emphasizing how we all have ups and downs; make a picture storybook or written narrative of a child's adventures; create a video or photo montage of a child's work on a project, an adventure, a family vacation, or a school achievement.

EXHIBIT I.1.
Five-Step Developmentally Focused Behavior Management*

1. "Is it important?" If not, ignore it. Keep focused on what's important for safety, attachment, and skill development. If it is important, first calm yourself (e.g., use "SOS"** Ford, Mahoney & Russo, 2003), then consider:
2. How old is the child acting developmentally?
3. Have traumas shaped the child's stress reactions? If so, what happened, especially at the developmental age the child is acting?
4. How could you respond to the child at the child's developmental age without any words and in a way that shows you can protect the child from past traumas, especially any fears of abandonment, violence, or harm to family members?
5. Until child calms down, say only what is necessary to show you can listen to child, that you understand the child's feelings and perspective, even if these are different than your own, and that you will maintain safety. Later, use the incident to help the child learn, at the child's developmental age, to replace old behaviors learned in the tough times.

Above all, avoid reenacting the child's traumas.

*Adapted from Dr. John Abbuhl's Three-Step Discipline for Difficult Behaviors (Abbuhl, J. Personal Communication).

**Ford, J.D., Mahoney, K., & Russo, E. (2003). TARGET *Trauma Adaptive Recovery Group Education and Therapy (9 Session Version) Leader Guide and Participant Handouts.* Farmington, CT: University of Connecticut Health Center. (www.ptsdfreedom.com).

Pitfalls

- Parents or guardians break pledges to create safety from repetitions of past traumas and child perceives that therapist and other significant adults tacitly accept this or fail to develop viable safety plans and help everyone involved grieve lost days and setbacks.
- Parents or guardians are unable physically or psychologically to raise child as primary caretakers, but this is not addressed in permanency work.
- Parents or guardians use rejection, threats of placement, and time-outs away from the family as discipline, triggering child's traumatic stress reactions to reminders of past losses, rejections, or abandonment.

Troubleshooting

If . . .	Then . . .
Difficulty engaging parents and potential caring adults	Check for shame-based messages perceived by caring adults and reinforce understanding of trauma as a framework to move beyond shame and blame. See *Families in Perpetual Crisis* (Kagan & Schlosberg, 1989) for detailed guidelines and case examples for engaging family members through home-based family therapy and family preservation programs. See *Turmoil to Turning Points: Building Hope for Children in Crisis Placements* (Kagan, 1996) for guidelines and case examples illustrating engagement of family members when children are in foster care, crisis, or mental health placements.
Adult **resists sharing**	Stress critical role of family members to help child heal from trauma by modeling the courage to share. Also, stress important role of family members to help child learn from family's heritage.
	Ensure that family members experience respect from therapists and agency staff for the importance of parents, grandparents, family values, a family's religion, and ethnicity.
	Watch for unspoken concerns about sharing family secrets with therapist and assess need for court orders of protection when adults or children have been threatened.
Children remind caring adults of their own traumas	When adults are triggered by children, offer individual trauma therapy for adults regarding their own traumatic life experiences. Work with caring adults to accentuate how they have made their lives different from the past and how they can utilize their understanding and resources as adults to keep themselves and their children safe. Use *TARGET* (Ford & Russo, 2006). Refer for individual therapy if individual work with adults is not possible.
Caretakers find it **too difficult to talk about their own past** but are supportive of their children	Encourage caring adults to support children's life story work including helping children learn about their past, strengths from their family heritage, and examples of family members' courage and efforts to overcome adversity. After children complete their life storybooks, encourage caring adults to work on their own issues.

If . . .	Then . . .
Children do not trust adults and repeatedly test or provoke adults	Watch for secret fears of child requiring additional safety plans. Help adults understand that child needs to see that these adults are different than the adults who hurt the child, or that adults have truly changed. Help parent practice how to respond to children to rebuild trust by: • Listening to child and respect for child's perceptions and memories • Validation of child's experiences • Stress on how their lives are different now • Safety messages • Supportive tone of voice, facial looks, touch • Modeling adding words to feelings
Children are in placement and **lack a permanency plan** including responsibilities for caring adults,	Trauma therapy often requires work by adults on building safety from domestic violence, physical abuse, sexual abuse, and neglect. Trauma work also requires time frames and plan for how children, adults, therapists, and authorities will monitor and know if changes are taking place. Therapists need to be well versed in permanency work and how to engage authorities, law guardians, and family court judges to implement an attachment-centered therapy that meets the requirements of the Adoption and Safe Families Act (see Kagan, 2004b, Chapter 5).
Parents or other designated **guardians are unsafe**	Within the context of state and federal requirements and mandates from family courts and child protective services (CPS), therapists should respect the right of adults to voice their own needs and their right to establish their own pace on working to provide safety for a child and overcome problems that have led to placement, court orders, or CPS monitoring. Parents have to keep themselves safe. At the same time, it is important for everyone to hear in meetings, conferences, and sessions that children need to be protected by other designated adults until parents can rebuild connections and demonstrate to CPS and family courts that they are keeping children safe.
Parents or other designated guardians are **unable to care for child safely** over extended period of time	Respecting the right of parents to choose what they can and will do also means working overtly with the children's inability to wait for long periods of time for parents to change and become capable or willing to parent a child to maturity. As part of trauma therapy, therapists need to be strong enough to help children and parents grieve when parents are unable to protect, provide, and guide (James, 1994) children. Children may need to be raised to maturity by a back-up guardian if parents cannot do what is necessary. Attachment and trauma therapy means voicing the child's need for permanency (Kagan & Schlosberg, 1989; Kagan, 1996, 2004b).

Checkpoints

_____ Caring adults utilize an understanding of their children's developmental level and experiences of trauma to eliminate any shaming and labeling of children and themselves.

_____   Caring adults develop and practice steps for care and protection of themselves to prevent reenactments of traumas.

_____   Caring adults begin their own life story work and address key points in the *Real Life Heroes* workbook including:

- Self-description of strengths, skills, and interests.
- Acceptance, recognition, and expression of feelings without losing control or hurting others.
- Heroes/Heroines: models, mentors, how helped others, guides to affect management.
- Important people in their lives: who nurtured, guided, protected adults at different ages, people they enjoy being with, people they want to visit.
- Positive memories with significant people.
- Self-soothing images, activities, and experiences.
- Genograms and time lines identifying important events, moves, transitions.
- Lessons learned to overcome tough times ranging from small problems to the hardest times including:
  — How the caring adult has learned to help others.
  — How the caring adult has made up for mistakes and harm to others.
  — Acceptance of own feelings and experiences, lessons learned, and goals for the future for self and family.
  — Integration of lessons learned and values from the past to the present.
  — Stress on how caring adults have made their lives safe from past problems and how their homes are now different than when children and parents experienced "tough times."

_____   Adults' life stories are shared in a way that helps children learn from caring adults without overburdening or traumatizing child with adults' experiences.

Safety Steps

Objectives

Engage caring adults to demonstrate that they will keep children safe by:

- Giving the child support and permission to share what the child experienced.
- Validating the child's experiences, including traumas involving the caring adult.
- Committing themselves to protecting child from anyone, even other family members the caring adult loves.
- Identifying how they see the child as special and part of their life.
- Demonstrating to children they are able to manage exposure to reminders of past traumas and manage their own reactions without retraumatizing children so that they will keep themselves and children safe when children share memories.
- Demonstrating commitment to: protect, nurture, and guide (James, 1989, 1994).
- Completing their own *Real Life Heroes* life storybook, or a substitute life story that includes a coherent narrative addressing Checkpoints.

Overview

Therapists can often engage caring adults by stressing how relationships with caring, committed adults are essential for children to overcome traumas. Children with traumatic stress have often learned that adults cannot be trusted, that safety pledges by adults in homes, at school, or in the community are not kept, and that real change is often an illusion filled with broken promises.

Caring adults become the heroes children need by demonstrating that they can become stronger than children's fears and nightmares. By so doing, caring adults help children become heroes themselves.

Adults begin to demonstrate their commitment is real by overcoming the "monsters" in their own lives including traumas that limited a parent's ability to care for, hear, validate, or protect a child. By completing their own versions of the *Real Life Heroes* life storybook, caring adults model courage and confidence that children need to persevere.

The success of this workbook relies largely on the ability of the adults to show that children will truly be safe to share. For a child, this means the adults involved will accept the child's perceptions and feelings as real for the child and will help the child to overcome distressing and shameful problems. This begins with the "Pledge" at the beginning of the book in which adults signify that they want the child to share what the child thinks, remembers, and feels. Children need to see that caring adults have the courage and ability to make this pledge a reality and that they do not have to fear losing a parent or any further abuse, neglect, or violence as a result of their disclosures.

Children cannot be expected to work on life stories if they are being asked to deny their experiences or to return to a home or school marked by violence or threats of rejection. Similarly, children cannot be expected to utilize life stories for positive growth if the adults around them do

Real Life Heroes: Practitioner's Manual
Published by The Haworth Press, Inc., 2007. All rights reserved.
doi:10.1300/5639_04

not have the courage to speak honestly about what has happened and to take responsibility for their own actions. Children learn how to deal with the truth from the adults who care enough to make a difference in their lives.

Subtle or covert pressure by adults to say or "remember" certain events in a certain way will lead to greater constriction in children and could generate false memories that distort children's understanding and accelerate behavior problems. If children show any signs of feeling pressured to say or remember events to please a family member, foster parent, or other significant adult, a neutral therapist should address this issue and work with family members and other service providers to develop and implement safety plans before children are asked to share any revealing information.

Step by Step

Working with the storybook and use of the manual should be directed by skilled trauma therapists (psychologists, social workers, or psychiatrists). For children in placement, foster parents or child care workers who have been trained in trauma therapy (See S.T.A.R.T., Benamati, 2004) also play critical roles in providing support and guidance.

Therapists serve as "witnesses" (Herman, 1992) and guides for the journey ahead, someone who is able to experience and also to contain the chaotic dysregulation of a child and family with traumatic stress. To do this, therapists need training, supervision, and support for attachment and trauma therapy. This is especially important whenever children have experienced events in which they feared someone would be seriously harmed or die, and when children appear agitated, lose awareness of what is happening around them, or act in ways that put themselves or others at risk of being hurt. When children are in foster or adoptive families, it is important that therapists are also knowledgeable about the experience of placement, permanency laws, and critical issues in adoption.

Before working with children, therapists are urged to complete the *Real Life Heroes* workbook, utilizing the flexibility and creativity suggested for work with children and adults and monitoring themselves for triggers and any needed work on self-protection.

Utilize individual sessions to begin work with potential caring adults and children with the understanding that children's work will be shared when safe, with the child's consent, and with protection established for each disclosure. Confidentiality, as in all therapeutic work, is limited by requirements to report neglect and abuse or dangers to children and adults to appropriate authorities. Separate sessions for children are essential until parents/guardians validate children's experiences of trauma and implement viable safety plans.

Develop, implement, and practice safety plans to address all known threats to children and caring adults and triggers leading to trauma reactions.

Safety plans need to include:

- identification of triggers and indicators leading to past crises;
- strategies prepared in advance to help caring adults and children stay in control;
- a list of names and phone numbers of safe, caring adults children can contact in every part of the day: at school, afterschool programs, at home, etc.;
- what each adult and child can do to prevent another cycle of violence; and
- demonstrations that safety plans will be implemented.

The therapist and child privately work out a nonverbal signal for child to indicate when he or she needs to stop (after Shapiro, 2001). Children must feel free to be able to signal or say "Stop, I need to take a break" and then be able to utilize some form of distraction, imagery, tension release, physical exercise, prayer, or meditation to soothe themselves.

Therapists need to be able to keep themselves as well as children safe. Therapists should develop and implement their own safety plan including awareness of their own triggers, ongoing consultation, and assistance from supervisors.

At the beginning of work, it is helpful to normalize how intense feelings are a normal part of healing. Remembering past events can rekindle both happy and painful feelings including sadness, loneliness, or anger. It is also natural for a child (or adult) to sometimes remember other events after sessions. This can be presented as a natural process in developing strength as a person and mastering old problems.

Development of safety plans often needs to include fostering recognition of different feelings by children and caring adults and identification of behaviors that signal an impending crisis. This can be addressed in Chapter 1 in the workbook as part of separate sessions with children and caring adults.

Once safety steps have been implemented, caring adults can be invited to join children at the end of sessions for children. Or, when beneficial, caring adults can join children in sessions. Caring adults will optimally be involved in work from workbook Chapters 3 through 8, although children and therapists should have the option at all times of using separate sessions to foster creativity. Special feedback/sharing sessions often work best with many children and the busy schedules of caring adults.

For children in placement because of abuse or neglect, essential safety steps need to include messages to the children from the first days of placement which are repeated at review conferences (see Kagan, 2004b) including:

- What needs to happen to restore safety and caring in their families.
- What will be done to help their parents.
- What their parents are doing to work on reuniting.
- A back-up (concurrent) plan if parents are unable or unwilling to work on reuniting.
- Who will keep the children safe during placement.
- What the children can do (their job) while they wait, e.g., go to school, learn skills, continue sports, hobbies, music, etc., and learn how to succeed, become responsible, and help others.

Pitfalls

- Omitting an individual evaluation with children that addresses safety concerns, triggers for trauma reactions, and attachments including what children need in order to feel safe with significant adults in their lives.
- Conducting trauma therapy sessions with parents or other adults in the room who have not met safety criteria.

Troubleshooting

If . . .	Then . . .
Child is **not safe to share**	Focus work with child in individual sessions on developing affect management skills and learning from child's heroes (workbook Chapters 1 and 2). Use workbook Chapters 3 and 4 to help search for caring adults who can help the child become safe enough to share.

If . . .	Then . . .
Child appears **anxious**	Therapists and caring adults can help a child relax by learning what helps each child. A hug from a trusted family member, a pat on the back, and praise for the child's courage may be all that is needed to help a child begin this work. Facial expressions, gestures, and the tone of a caring adult's voice are critical in establishing permission to work with a therapist. For other children, frequent breaks, physical activities, or repeated practice in deep breathing, imagery, and relaxation techniques with a therapist may be necessary.
Children show **acute signs of stress**	Children showing signs of acute stress often need intensive services including close supervision in order to feel safe at home, at school, or in their neighborhoods. The workbook was not designed for use with schizophrenic children who do not have the capacity to separate fantasy from reality, or for high-risk children who cannot be kept safe enough to manage the anxiety created by addressing family experiences.
A **comprehensive assessment is not available**	Refer for comprehensive psychological evaluations to identify attachments, risks, unspoken threats, obstacles, subtle triggers, and to develop viable safety plans and services.
Implementation of **safety plans** is **not certain**	Check on whether safety plans have been implemented by asking if everyone involved, from children to parents, grandparents, extended family members, school officials, and authorities, can share what will be done to keep children (and adults) safe from repetitions of past traumas at home, in their neighborhoods, and at school: • Who will do what? • What will signal that a crisis cycle is starting again? • Who can serve as protectors from outside the nuclear family to guard against any further abuse or neglect? • Who is committed to protecting the children, even if it means confronting parents or calling CPS? • How can protectors be contacted? • Do children have their phone numbers? • Who will check on children to maintain safety and how often must this happen in order to keep children safe?
Parents cannot manage affect regulation or reactions to reminders of traumas	Often, parents need to show children they are working on overcoming their own traumas in order to help their children. This may involve extended, or even lifelong therapy. Use TARGET (Ford & Russo, 2006) materials and adults work on their own skill development; their own life stories as well as Chapter 25 can help begin this process.
Parents care about their child but **are not able or willing to validate their child's experiences**	Parents who care about their child but are not able or willing to validate their child's experiences may still be able to give support for therapeutic work in concrete ways, e.g., giving permission for a child to work on the life storybook privately with the therapist, purchasing colored pencils or markers, or providing paper for drawings, etc.

If . . .	Then . . .
Parents appear unable or unwilling to take on the full task of raising a child or to overcome the impact of traumas on the child	It is important to respect how parents demonstrate their choices hour by hour and day by day in terms of making the changes necessary to create safe homes, rebuild attachments, and care for children. Reassessing commitment of family members can also be helpful to clarify capacity to change, obstacles to change, perceived mandates from the family, their culture, communities, and authorities, and assistance that could be provided.
Parents stop working on change **or fail to make necessary changes** within ASFA time limits for children in placement	Parents may feel they need to avoid change or move slowly over many years to stop risky behaviors and overcome traumas in their lives. Children, however, don't have the time to wait without suffering extensive impairment of their own development. Therapists can help parents, children, extended family members, and caring adults to voice both successes and failures, grieve what cannot be changed, and at all times promote the best possible relationship between a parent and a child. Please see Kagan and Schlosberg (1989) and Kagan (1996) for detailed guidelines for permanency work.
Parent insists other parent is all bad and blocks child from learning about other parent, **parent alienation syndrome**	Watch for signs in child's or parent's nonverbal reactions that talking about a missing parent is not allowed. Use workbook Chapters 3 and 4 to open up learning by child about other parent. Stress how research has shown that children need to know the good things each parent has done, as well as the bad. When parents separate, children do best when they can have the best possible relationship with each parent and when the child's needs are placed above the grievances of either parent.
Parent "loves" child but **will not allow child to be seen alone**	Attempt to meet with parent alone to address concerns and develop safety plans that reassure parent that therapist respects the caring parent, and will support 'love' of parent and child while helping child to overcome presenting problems and achieve goals. Divide sessions between parent and child, meeting first with parent, and then child. If necessary, limit individual time at first to a few minutes and gradually expand.
Parent **limits what child can say or talk about**	Address injunctions to not talk about certain issues as important communications from parent about where safety plans are needed. Injunctions may stem from parent's own history of being hurt and rules parent developed to protect self and child from abuse or abandonment. If possible, work with parent to frame goals as promoting child's strengths including the ability to see, hear, and voice what is real while maintaining respect and caring for parent.
	In some cases, it may be helpful for parents to complete the workbook with the therapist before starting work with child.
Child **fears parent will relapse**, especially during certain times in the year	Children's distress and threat avoidance will naturally escalate during time periods when parents have relapsed in the past, returning to drug use, neglect, etc. Holidays and anniversary dates of losses often mark times when children become especially anxious and preoccupied with recurrence of past traumas. When this occurs, it is helpful to focus directly on what can help children to know that a parent is safe (after Macy, Barry & Gill, 2003). What could help a child to relax, even for a second, knowing that parent is safe?

If . . .	Then . . .
	Signals of relapse can be built into safety plans, e.g., number of cigarettes or cups of coffee consumed, ability of parent to laugh when tickled by a feather, parent fixing breakfast for child, parent spending time with positive friends, going to NA, or having random drug checks by an authority.

Checkpoints

_____ Safety plans are developed and implemented to protect children from threats of violence, emotional abuse, or neglect and for known triggers to children's trauma reactions.

_____ Before children are asked to share workbook materials with caring adults in or out of sessions, caring adults demonstrate that they have met the safety criteria listed under objectives.

In addition, before joint sessions are started:

_____ Child indicates in private to therapist that child feels safe to share with caring adult present and wants the caring adult in sessions.

_____ Child demonstrates ability and willingness to signal to therapist and other protective adults if child, at any time, feels unsafe with caring adult present.

The Pledge:
Beginning the Adventure

Objectives

- Provide orientation to children and caring adults on session structure, safety guidelines, and format of the workbook.
- Develop plan to identify and strengthen capacity of a primary *and* a back-up parent figure for children who are in placement or at high risk of placement.
- Invite caring adults to sign the "Pledge," explicitly giving children permission to share, and committing adults to validate children's experiences and to work separately on their own life story.
- Invite children to print names in first sentence of the "Pledge" and begin the workbook with therapist in individual sessions.
- Arrange for mentor to help develop creative arts or other special skills whenever possible.

Overview

This is where the journey begins for both children and caring adults. The hero metaphor provides a means to engage children in a shared quest, using creative arts activities to work, step by step, with a therapist to build skills and confidence. In this context, life story work can be introduced as an adventure. The therapist serves as a guide, committed to helping children and caring adults overcome whatever obstacles lie ahead. The *Real Life Heroes* workbook provides the structure for keeping the quest safe and moving forward, utilizing activities to foster success and over time to reshape beliefs and behaviors that have hindered a child's development.

Therapists can encourage children and caring adults to utilize the workbook to uncover or strengthen special "qualities" in themselves, in their families, and in the people who care (or cared) about them—the special qualities that have helped them through good times and bad. In this way, life story work becomes an invitation to regain power in their lives. For traumatized children and adults, this means moving from a history of victimization to an understanding of oneself as a hero in one's own story, and to enlarge this story with a past, a present, and a future.

As in all quests, it helps to work with a safe and trustworthy mentor, someone who models for a child how it is possible to overcome problems and who recognizes special qualities in the child. The therapist serves as a mentor but also as a guide to the larger quest. When children are living apart from biological parents, foster parents or extended family members can also become important mentors. Engage the child to develop his or her special talents with a mentor who can function outside of the family and therapy sessions. It is not necessary that a mentor know exactly how a child can succeed, but rather, a mentor shows a child that there is a way out of difficult situations, and that what may seem hopeless can be solved. Mentors can be paid or volunteers recruited by therapists already part of a child's life. Relatives or older siblings can of-

Real Life Heroes: Practitioner's Manual
Published by The Haworth Press, Inc., 2007. All rights reserved.
doi:10.1300/5639_05

ten provide mentoring for children. Clergy, coaches, drama teachers, local musicians, and skilled craftspeople may also provide mentoring. Caring adults can also serve as mentors.

Ideally, mentors are people who have experienced some of the adversity affecting a child and have found ways to utilize their experiences to foster special skills. The mentor can then pass along these special skills, enabling a child to succeed. In keeping with the theme of heroes, mentors can be asked to facilitate a child's sharing what he or she learned in the future with others.

A temporary mentor and a therapist, however, are insufficient when children lack a safe home and a nurturing adult committed to raising them to maturity. For children in placement or who lack a safe home with a nonoffending, caring and committed guardian, the first step in the quest is rebuilding a sense of hope. Service plans and therapeutic goals often need to explicitly target searching for, finding, and strengthening relationships between children and safe, caring, committed adults.

Signing the "Pledge" represents a contract between the therapist, mentors, and primary guardians. The Pledge marks the beginning of the quest and the starting point for the child to test whether these adults will really work to make the child's world safe enough for the child to tell his or her story.

Step by Step

Introduce the *Real Life Heroes* workbook to caring adults and children as a series of activities that have helped many children and caring adults who have experienced stress or traumas. Activities utilize creative arts (drawing, rhythm, music, movement, photos, and stories) to:

- Identify interests, talents, wishes, and heroes for each child and caring adult.
- Foster an understanding of how traumas impact children and adults and how we can develop skills to cope with tough times.
- Tell the story of a child's life, accentuating strengths for the child, his or her family, and ethnic heritage.
- Detoxify traumas from the past including losses and experiences of violence. Help traumatized children and adults become stronger, establish safety in their lives, and feel better about themselves by building on their growing skills and relationships to create a better future.

Establish prerequisites for all sessions including:

- Child's disclosures will remain confidential and in accordance with laws requiring reporting of abuse and neglect.
- Parents and caring adults involved in any sessions are committed to protecting the child (see Safety Steps, page 56).
- Child and caring adults are able to signal when feeling unsafe, e.g., snapping fingers, blinking three times, raising a hand.
- Child is able to manage the stress of working in therapy without dangerous behavior.
- Signatures below the Pledge indicate affirmation of these principles.

Begin mentoring, where possible, in an area of interest, e.g., music, theater arts, art, or sports, to promote expressive skills, confidence, and self-esteem. Mentoring is especially important for children who have fewer than three safe, caring adults committed to helping children now and into adulthood.

Mentors need to commit to, minimally, a six-month relationship. Mentoring works best when children can continue to work with a mentor for several years and to maturity ideally. Mentors should have training in understanding trauma and trauma behaviors as well as preparation and ongoing consultation at least once a month with the child's therapist on how to deal with predictable trauma-related behaviors.

When children are in placement, or are at risk of placement, help them identify wishes for a primary and a back-up plan to find a parent figure who could raise them to maturity. Demonstrate in permanency planning meetings how the child's needs and wishes help frame a concurrent permanency plan.

When therapists know that children have experienced specific traumas, e.g., a hurricane, the death of a parent in a car accident, or sexual molestation by an uncle, it is important that children *hear* that therapists, and whenever possible, caring adults, *validate in words* what the child has shared. In a neutral manner, therapists can simply state that they understand that the children experienced, for instance, Hurricane _____, the death of their father in a car accident, or sexual abuse by Uncle _____.

Introduce *Real Life Heroes* as a workbook that has helped many children to make their lives better by building strengths and making it easier to share what happened in a safe way. The workbook will be used to help children become stronger so they can feel better after difficult experiences. This message should occur at the beginning of therapy so that children understand how the workbook will help them. Not linking the workbook to the child's experiences also risks that traumatized children will perceive that therapists and caring adults don't really believe what the child has shared, that these adults are too frightened or weak to help with what happened, or, that the child is just too bad or damaged to be helped.

Tell children that they can work slowly or quickly on the workbook. In pilot studies, the workbook was completed in twenty to fifty sessions, six to eighteen months. The length of time varies with the safety, stability, age of onset and chronicity of traumas, type and level of attachments, length of time for sessions (sixty to ninety minutes), home-based versus clinic-based work, caseload for therapists, and resources available for the child and family.

Therapists can use the manual as a framework to keep therapy moving forward beyond work on the "crisis de jour," while fostering creativity and security for each child. Some children require many sessions and additional exercises to develop the ability to identify and express feelings without losing control. With children in foster care, a great deal of detective work may be needed just to collect facts regarding moves and reasons for moves in the child's life (workbook Chapter 7). Other children will need multiple sessions in order to develop the safety to tell the story of their "toughest time" in Chapter 8. The "Troubleshooting" section for each workbook chapter provides tips on helping children who require additional assistance.

Introduce to children and parents a plan for review conferences to help keep the trauma work moving. Review conferences should address:

- child and parent/guardian goals for rebuilding or building safety, attachments, and skills to replace misbehavior, preventing unnecessary placements, reuniting children in placement with families, or finding alternate families for children in placement who cannot return home;
- progress toward goals including safety, trust, and skills to succeed at home, school, and in the community;
- obstacles/problems;
- what led up to problems;
- what can be done to overcome problems; and
- action plans.

Children, and, especially adolescents, should be encouraged to indicate caring adults they would like to have present at review conferences. Caring adults can be involved as necessary by teleconferencing, videoconferencing, or with follow-up telephone calls if they cannot be present.

Schedule review conferences to occur at least every eight weeks. When children are in placement, review conferences are needed every four to six weeks to keep work moving forward on rebuilding attachments, to establish and maintain safety, to meet federal and state requirements (e.g., the Adoption and Safe Families Act), and to maintain hope for a child. For detailed guidelines, please see *Families in Perpetual Crisis* (Kagan & Schlosberg, 1989) and *Rebuilding Attachments with Traumatized Children* (Kagan, 2004b).

Pitfalls

- Child perceives primary caretakers or family members mandating limited responses or denial of traumas and that this is accepted or supported by therapists and other caring adults.
- Child is living in an unsafe home and safety plans are not developed.
- Child living in placement has heard a message from parents, extended family members, and authorities that child must return to an unsafe home.
- Child is living in placement and does not have, or is not aware of, a viable "permanency plan" including a back-up (concurrent) plan for finding and strengthening substitute guardians in case primary caretakers are unable or unwilling to do what is necessary to protect and care for child to maturity.

Troubleshooting

If . . .	Then . . .
Child **lacks any safe and validating parent**	Introduce *Real Life Heroes* as a means to search for caring adults, especially adults willing and able to parent the child to maturity. After identifying possible caring adults, the next step is to develop and implement viable safety plans, step by step. Invite child to work simultaneously with *Real Life Heroes* materials and a supportive team of therapists and hopefully extended family members, to identify and find two to three caring adults who can support the child, even if some can't raise a child in their homes. Working on pages of the life storybook, especially Chapter 3, is very useful in providing information on who a therapist can contact. The emphasis in this work should not be on the child finding caring adults, but rather the therapist, collaterals, and extended family members, where possible, working with information the child shares to find and strengthen potential caretakers for the child.
Child has **only one identified caring adult** who the child can count on for support, validation, and protection	Tell the child, that it's important to identify a back-up plan and to work on both plans at the same time. This is true whether you are running a candy store, acting as president, or writing a life storybook about families. That means identifying at least two possible caring adults, so that if the first adult can't or won't do what is necessary to help, the therapist (and other staff) will work on helping the child develop a relationship with another adult. The child can be asked very simply, "Who could help _____ (primary parent-figure) to take care of you?" Or, "who would you like to live with, if _____ (primary parent figure) for some reason, can't take care of you?"

If . . .	Then . . .
Child is living in placement and **lacks a permanency plan** that the child can believe will lead to a safe, nurturing home	Introduce *Real Life Heroes* as a means to identify caring adults willing to work on building trust with the child. This can include invitations to parents, extended family members, and other adults to work on validating a child and helping the child to become stronger. Viability of permanency plans should be assessed from the child's perspective and include safety plans to prevent or protect the child from repetitions of previous traumas. For detailed guidelines on permanency work and case examples, please see *Rebuilding Attachments with Traumatized Children* and *Turmoil to Turning Points: Building Hope in Crisis Placements* (Kagan, 1996, 2004b).
Child **cannot manage living in a family,** or older adolescent refuses to consider family living	Group care or independent living programs are never sufficient as a back-up plan by themselves; however, for adolescents who have demonstrated, over multiple years and family placements, that they cannot manage family living, e.g., fifteen- to sixteen-year-olds who refuse to consider family living, *Real Life Heroes* materials can be used to identify caring adults who would be willing and able to support youths living in supervised programs. This should include helping the youth in a crisis, or someone the youth could call, if necessary, in the middle of the night.
Child has **two caring adults but loses one,** e.g., a parent figure becomes incarcerated	It's important to directly address the child's loss and the need for minimally two, and ideally, at least three caring adults committed to the child. If one caretaker is temporarily lost due to illness, stress, other responsibilities, or jail, it's helpful to follow steps listed previously for a child with just one caring adult. In many cases, both the remaining caring adult and the adult who is leaving can be enlisted to help find another caring adult to help the child during a temporary absence. And, whether or not the absence is temporary, it will be important to help the child, and any caring adults, to grieve this loss.

Checkpoints

_____ Child can name caring adults who have pledged to help the child, keep the child safe from a recurrence of past or feared traumas, and respect whatever the child shares in his or her life storybook, even criticism of the caring adults.

_____ If child can identify fewer than two caring adults, child understands that *Real Life Heroes* will be used to search for and find caring adults willing to help.

_____ Therapist demonstrates the courage to address any "demons" that the child and the child's family have experienced including validating known experiences of past traumas and "saying the words."

_____ Therapist arranges for support, training, safety for themselves, and ongoing consultation to face the challenges ahead.

Structuring Sessions: Guiding the Child

Objectives

Introduce child and caring adults to the format for sessions including:

- Use of Knots and Personal Power Thermometers
- Safety checks
- Use of Magical Moments and Centering Exercises
- Use of creative arts with workbook pages:
  — Sketch
  — Tap rhythm
  — Add two-to-three note chord
  — Try out action pose
  — Answer questions
  — Opportunity to develop each page into a story with a beginning, middle, and end
- Ending sessions with repeated use of Thermometers and Centering
- Involvement of caring adults in sessions when possible
- Opportunities, when safety criteria are met, to share work with safe adults
- Extra activities after sessions
- Expectations and management of natural reactions after sessions
- Schedule of sessions

Overview

All journeys need preparation, tools, and rituals to promote confidence and ensure success. To promote a child's trust, therapists are encouraged to develop a routine for each session that highlights how these are special times. Life story work can become a magical time for children. Therapists and parents can set the mood by working with children in a comfortable and quiet setting, minimizing distractions, and offering limited choices to give children a sense of control. Serving a sweet, herbal tea or hot cocoa and a special kind of cookie, creates an aroma and taste that conveys comfort and support. Allowing children to select their favorite herbal tea or juice each day, reading the label and choosing the taste, smell, and attributes they want, e.g., "calming," or "invigorating," helps empower and soothe children from the inside out. A brief centering exercise and a "Magical Moment" help to make these sessions special.

The room utilized should be become a sanctuary from the child's stress, protected by the therapist and any caring adults who are invited to participate. Predictability, respect for safety, and routines help children develop confidence that caring adults will keep them safe, and in turn, renew confidence that energy spent on threat detection, hypervigilance, and avoidance can be at least temporarily reduced within this special time.

Real Life Heroes: Practitioner's Manual
Published by The Haworth Press, Inc., 2007. All rights reserved.
doi:10.1300/5639_06

In group and foster family care programs, it works best to separate the roles of case planners/managers from therapists and caring adults. Children and caring adults will naturally bring the day's or week's most pressing issues to the case manager; extra effort and time will be needed by the case manager to separate therapy time from management of case planning, permanency, milieu, foster parent supervision, and other day-to-day management issues. It is also important to maintain the "sanctuary" of the special times set aside for children's appointments, even when other children are acting out their distress. When one therapist must bear responsibility for both case management and therapy sessions, it has worked well to bring in interns or family support workers who can take on the clinical work for children and families under supervision of a trained clinician. Making therapy sessions predictable and safe in group care, foster family care, and school-based programs requires endorsement and implementation by administrators, supervisors, staff, and clients of core principles of trauma therapy including protection, maintaining therapy sessions, respect for staff, children, and families, and incorporation of democratic values to make the organization a Sanctuary (Bloom, 1997).

Trauma therapy is hard work. The session structure was designed to promote enjoyable activities and to foster children's creativity through music, art, and movement. This process accentuates nonverbal meaning and exposure time for nonverbal processing before working on re-integration with words. The workbook pages in each chapter begin with relatively innocuous items and build to somewhat more challenging questions. Therapists are encouraged to be creative in how they utilize written questions. Therapists can adapt the workbook to best facilitate each child's interests and talents and to utilize the therapist's own talents and enjoyment of art and music. For example, for a child who likes to dance, the Action Movement part of the sequence could be emphasized for storytelling.

Traumatized children learn healing is possible within caring relationships that foster safety and trust the child's world has truly changed. Typically, children need to test whether change is real. This often means provoking the adults around them to repeat what was unbearable during past traumas. Testing works best when adults are off guard or struggling with other stressors, e.g., problems with the landlord, at work, the car breaking down, an argument between parents. That's when children find out how much parents, family members, guardians, and mentors really care and what is real.

Since children are especially traumatized by the breakdown of their ability to trust parents and guardians, testing will, in most cases, involve provoking caring adults to enact past traumas. With an understanding of trauma and children's past experiences, therapists and caring adults can welcome or even prescribe testing by children. Testing can be discussed and planned as homework, a way to validate the child's need to find out if his or her life is really different. Testing can be used as a way to practice recognition of triggers and signs that mark the beginning of trauma cycles. No caring adult should expect to be perfect. Testing can be encouraged by caring adults to demonstrate their awareness of dangers and triggers for children, their commitment to implement safety plans, how they accept responsibility for what they do, even when they make mistakes, and how they will work to reattach when gaps begin to form between children and adults.

For therapists, testing by children often involves distractions that disrupt progress on the workbook or the sequence of sessions. This is often a test of the sanctuary of therapy sessions and whether therapists can be coaxed or provoked to stop work on overcoming traumas. Therapists, like all caring adults, do not have to be perfect. Therapists need to use their own supports and awareness of trauma patterns. Then, they can demonstrate how safety rules will be maintained and that work on building strengths will continue, even during difficult times for a child, a family, or the therapist.

Step by Step

Demonstrate how sessions are special times with a predictable order including:

1. Welcoming messages.
2. Safety assurances: review of the "Pledge" and "Safety Steps" including how the child can signal when something is too toxic to address and demonstration that therapist will watch and listen for this signal, respecting the child's capacity. Therapists can come back to pages or tasks at a later time in the work when a child is more secure.
3. Self-ratings of stress (Knots), self-control (Personal Power), and feelings of mad, sad, and glad. Introduce Knots as feelings of tightness, tension, or even aching all over the body. Personal power means using your whole body. That means being able to sense how you're feeling from the tip of your toes to the thinking power of your brain. Personal power means self control so you can use your strength to help yourself and help others.

    Ask children to scan over their bodies from their toes to the top their heads, and then mark, or color in, the level on each thermometer from one to ten indicating how high they would rate that feeling at that moment.

    "My Thermometers" (Chapter 19) is used as a tool for "checking in" and also to develop the child's ability to self-monitor through practice each session. Use of the thermometers also fosters respect for the child's feelings, and provides reassurance that the therapist won't push the child beyond what the child can manage.

    If desired, an additional thermometer can be used to highlight an important attribute for a child. For instance, with a child who appears agitated, it is helpful to encourage a self-rating of their energy level from "exhausted" to "hyper."

The ratio of the child's "Personal Power" to "Knots" provides a quick measure of a child's capacity to manage stress at that moment. When the child's stress is equal to or greater than their feelings of self-control, it is important to focus work on safety issues, reducing distress, and enhancing self-control.

4. Focusing/centering exercise e.g., "safe place" imagery, balancing a peacock feather (Macy, Barry, & Gill, 2003) with deep breathing, a yoga exercise, deep belly breathing and muscle relaxation exercises (see workbook Chapter 2; self-soothing skills, page 55), blowing bubbles and modulating breath, winding oneself to one side, tensing and letting go.
5. Magical moment: show child a simple trick, experiment with tonality and sound with a glockenspiel (xylophone), point out mysteries of snowflakes falling down, repeat a dance or movement child has shown therapist, start session with a special seven-step handshake, blow a giant bubble, examine a gem or geode, etc. Using the German word, *glockenspiel,* adds a magical quality to even an inexpensive xylophone.
6. Workbook pages: typically one to three pages, depending on the difficulty for the child.
7. Repeating "Knots" and "Personal Power" thermometers at end of session: highlight increases in "Personal Power" and decreases in "Knots."
8. Safety planning and reassurance: to deal with predictable stressors before the next session including who the child can call at different times of the day and week if they feel stressed. Reassurance that any thoughts or feelings that come up after the session are to be expected and part of healing; the child can be asked to record anything that comes up or to share these, if possible, with a trusted adult who would be willing to record them and share with the therapist.
9. Between sessions: Whenever possible, encourage children (and caring adults) to practice self-soothing focusing/centering skills daily until they become automatic. In some cases,

children (and caring adults) can be asked to nonverbally sketch responses to additional workbook pages and then bring these in to the next session where the therapist can encourage sharing with the steps listed previously.

10. "Good-bye" message: including time/date for next session.

Use workbook pages to encourage nonverbal expression, to create opportunities for validation, and to promote attunement with children:

- Ask children to respond nonverbally to each page beginning with drawings as "silent stories" (Macy, Barry, & Gill, 2003) by selecting colors and then experimenting with sketches, accentuating intensity and detail.
- Add rhythm to a drawing by asking child to tap out the drawing as a beat, experimenting and shaping loudness and tempo to match the child's image. Children may enjoy constructing their own homemade drums with coffee cans and different covers tightened with string as well as experimenting with different drumsticks, glockenspiel mallets, etc.
- Experiment with tonality to go along with rhythm and images. This can be done in a simple manner by encouraging child to pick a note on the glockenspiel to go along with the image for each page. Later, children can be encouraged to develop the note into a three-note chord by adding notes to complement the first note selected. This could mean taking the "1, 3, 5" notes for a simple chord progression; however, the emphasis should be on fostering the child's safety and creativity to select notes desired to convey a musical story. Afterward, children could be encouraged to experiment with tempo, rhythm, and patterns with the notes in this chord.

    Creative music can be used as an opportunity to foster bonding with a child in much the same way that an infant or toddler learns to coo and make sounds and simple words through attunement with a caring parent who repeats what a child says. Attunement and harmony counter a child's feelings of isolation after traumas. It is very helpful for the therapist and, where possible, a caring adult, to begin by copying (echoing) the child's notes on the glockenspiel, then tapping the note in unison. Later, it may be possible to mirror, harmonize, or to accentuate the base note of the child's chord while the child experiments with notes, chords, and patterns (See Austin, 2002; Macy, Barry, & Gill, 2003).

- Encourage children to try out and assume an *"Action Pose."* Children (and parents) are familiar with action figures and how they can sometimes be adjusted to demonstrate an attitude and action using posture, facial appearance, and positioning its arms, hands, legs, torso, and neck. Similarly, with the Action Pose, ask children to enact what they have drawn on the workbook page with a gesture, a look, by how they position their arms, hands, or legs, or by a short movement to add richness to drawings and music.

    To facilitate the child's comfort with the Action Pose, invite the child to think of herself or himself as an actor working with the figures drawn on the page. Actors take on the feeling of a character and show it with their bodies through movement and action.

    Use a mirror (Mullin, 2004) or a camera to help children capture the look of the Action Pose. Remind them how actors also practice with mirrors and movie directors often try scenes several times, asking actors to try different movements to capture what they want to express. Children can also be asked to copy how they look in the mirror, as a drawing, to highlight what they are showing. Mirrors ideally should be large enough to reflect the child's upper body, if not a whole body stance.

- Provide child with opportunities for nonverbal processing of each page with enough time to accentuate positives engendered in each workbook page and to gain a positive sense of balance regarding the task. This should be reflected through reduced ratings of Knots and increased ratings of the child's Personal Power.

If children become distressed by workbook pages, especially for more difficult tasks in Chapters 7 and 8, check how the child would rate herself or himself on the Knots and Personal Power thermometers. Encourage the child to continue to use rhythm, music, or Action Poses along with self-soothing steps until child feels Knots Thermometer at a "3" or less and Personal Power Thermometer rating higher than their Knots. Part II, Chapter 9 of the Practitioner's Manual *introduces steps for teaching children deep breathing, "SOS" (Ford et al., 2003), safe place imagery, and thought stopping.*

- Invite children to add verbal responses to describe their drawing, rhythm, tonality, and Action Pose. Elicit thoughts, actions, and feelings, the "cognitive triangle" for every image.
- Reinforce child's success in conveying images, melodies, and stories, "silent" or verbal, for each page/task of workbook.
- Explore ways to make each page fun by linking to child's interests and talents and encouraging related activities with caring adults and opportunities to foster creative arts skills.
- Help children add meaning to pictures by adding a "before," an "after," and, if possible, a "lesson learned." This can easily be developed into stories in which child writes or nonverbally shares memories of events and a brief story highlighting what helped. Similarly, moving from single tones to chords can lead to a musical story; and, fixed action poses can be explored as movement stories. Visual, musical, and movement stories can be explored as efforts to cope, which may have been blocked during traumas (after Ogden, Minton, & Pain, 2006).
- Enrich stories by matching verbal guidance and questions to a child's developmental age, interests, and level of stress. Examples of facilitating questions include:
  — Draw a picture in your mind and focus, just for a minute, on what was happening.
  — Where would you be?
  — What is around you?
  — Who are you with?
  — What do they look like?
  — What are they doing? (For instance, How are they taking care of you?)
  — What is the expression on their face? What are they showing in their eyes, their mouth, lips, and their cheeks?
  — Focus on your sensations: touch, smell, sight, sounds. What are you feeling?
  — What are you doing in the picture?
  — What happened just before?
  — What happened next?
  — What would happen in the end?
  — What was the most important part of this story for you?
  — If you shared this story with another child, what would be the lesson the child could learn?
- Creativity and flexibility by the therapist and child is very important, and, it may be necessary to arrange special sessions to develop skills, e.g., self-soothing, or to arrange phone calls, special visits, or "detective" work in order to engage and learn from other family members, practitioners, teachers, or other resources for a child. After additional information is gained or skills and stability are established, therapists can return with the child to complete earlier sections.
- Encourage a caring adult who has met safety criteria to join child at the end of sessions. Any contact between adults and a child should be based on the child's comfort and trust with the child able to signal, or ask, at any time, for physical separation. Depending on the child's comfort, ask the caring adult to sit close as a support as child shares work completed. In some instances, it is helpful for the caring adult to gently put an arm behind a child. Some children may only be able to handle a gentle touch on their back for a second or

two at first, but gradually, over time, this can build to several seconds, and after several weeks or months, to a minute. This is often a significant reflection of the child's growing trust, especially if touch in the past had been associated with physical or sexual abuse or family violence.

- Beginning in workbook Chapter 3, encourage caring adult involvement at the end of sessions to assist children to learn about stories of family members caring for the child and strengths within the family including their ethnic heritage. For Chapter 7, interviews and contacts with caring adults are often necessary to learn about moves. This can provide a means for therapists and children to engage otherwise noninvolved family members.

- Provide time whenever possible for caring adults (see "Guardians and Mentors") to work on their own life story and trauma recovery work. Ideally, initial sessions would provide half the time for children and half for caring adults to work on their own issues. After caring adults have met safety criteria, the last ten to fifteen minutes of sessions could be used for sharing work completed by the child and reinforcement of the child's work by caring adults. In practice, this typically needs to be modified to match availability of adults and time/ funding restrictions.

- Encourage caring adults to accept, and where appropriate, to assign the child to "test" them over the course of several days; the child can assess how adults are making all of their lives safe and different. Children can be assigned homework to test whether a safety plan is being followed, e.g., by trying out a signal agreed upon that would lead to caring adults talking individually with children.

- Utilize "Session Summary/Progress Notes" (Chapter 21) to record progress and track fidelity.

- Provide child with a "Bookmark" (Chapter 22) to structure session format and mark progress through the workbook. The bookmark serves as a reminder list for sessions. Let children know that the idea for bookmarks came from a child completing the workbook. Encourage children to color in the back of the Bookmark. Afterward, bookmarks can be laminated.

Pitfalls

- Focusing sessions on resolving each day's biggest crisis instead of building skills and changing trauma reaction patterns.

- Child perceives therapist is afraid to confront details of memories, e.g., frightening aspects of an abusive adult's appearance or sexual abuse, inadvertently reinforcing the power of feared people and events.

- Rushing too quickly through workbook without taking time for skill building, strengthening, or building attachments, and emotional processing through integration of nonverbal creative arts and narratives. Or, repeated short exposures to difficult memories that do not allow sufficient time for child to practice affect modulation skills, to reduce distress tied to specific memories, or to gain a sense of self-control.

Troubleshooting

If . . .	Then . . .
Aggressive or self-destructive behaviors create safety risks	Refer children *and* parents separately to individual therapy to work on specific safety issues including anger management, domestic violence, substance abuse, child traumatic stress, adult PTSD, and mental health impairments with progress shared in review conferences.

If . . .	Then . . .
	When attachment-impaired children react to triggers with risky behaviors, appeal to their need to be in control. For instance, ask, "Where's your *Personal Power?* How are you using your brains, your strength, your skills, to reach your goals?" Later, ask, "What happened? What triggered your *Knots* going up? What would help? Who could help you?"
Children **lack self-soothing and affect modulation skills**	Provide extended practice sessions in developing self-soothing skills. Typically, this can be carried out in conjunction with affect regulation skill-building beginning in workbook Chapter 1. Additional skills can be fostered in work with caring adults with yoga and self-comforting exercises, e.g., cross arms up to shoulders, squeeze gently, rock self gently, tap shoulders lightly.
Children appear **constricted** in ability to express themselves	Check for secrets, unresolved safety risks, or threats. Mentoring in art or music is especially helpful to foster the comfort and basic skills needed for this work. This can also be encouraged for caring adults.
Children have been **abused or neglected** by parents	Placement is needed when children have been severely abused or neglected and parents or guardians fail to take necessary steps to validate children's experiences and develop viable safety plans that include monitoring by safe caring adults even if that means calling authorities and confronting parents or guardians. Identify at least three supportive and protective adults who will monitor and ensure safety for child, 24-7, until parents rebuild trust over an extended period of time. Monitoring needs to include checking in privately and individually with the child along with signals the child can use and test to bring in help. This may require months of monitoring for single incidents, or years, in cases of repeated abuse or neglect. In cases of severe and repeated abuse or neglect by parents and parents' refusal or failure to work on making necessary changes, children need to understand how state and federal laws, e.g., the Adoption and Safe Families Act, will be enforced by authorities and that children will not be sent back to violent homes or forced to go to visits that reinforce traumas (see Kagan, 2004b, regarding permanency work with abuse and neglect).
Conflicts develop between parents, foster parents, and other caring adults	Avoid splitting and fragmented work by involving parents, caring adults, therapists, and mentors in **collaborative planning** beginning with contracting sessions and continuing with regularly scheduled review conferences.
Therapist has **responsibility for both case management and trauma therapy**	Clarify with child how therapist will separate both of these special and important roles and, wherever possible, schedule a separate time and day for weekly *Real Life Heroes* sessions and use a different location. When that is not possible, therapist can tell child that in each meeting time, the therapist will split the session. The child can be asked, "Would you like to work on your *Real Life Heroes* book first or second?" It also helps to bring in a caring adult who will work on attunement and support for child in sessions. When no safe family members are available for this work, child care workers or foster parents can play a vital role as caring adults. See also guidelines of use of graduate student interns (outlined in the Introduction).

If . . .	Then . . .
Child is **excited or distressed about something** that happened or is about to happen, e.g., a fight at school, or an upcoming visit with a family member	Tell child that therapist will spend time with child on what happened, or is about to happen, along with regular special time to work on the *Real Life Heroes* materials. Therapist can split the session and emphasize that both are important. The child can be asked, "Would you like to work on your *Heroes* book first or second?"
Child begins session with a dramatic story that **leads parent to intervene to discipline** or protect child	Children may begin sessions with a story of an event or behavior that provokes parental intervention, especially when sessions are held in family homes. For instance, a child may talk about how the principal or a police officer came to see him in his classroom that day, or how the child needed to run away from a gang of kids on the way home from school. In these situations, it is helpful to acknowledge the child's story and then encourage the child and parent to slow down and utilize some of the calming and centering skills developed in earlier sessions, e.g., "SOS" (Ford & Russo, 2006), assuring both parent and child that the therapist will get back to deal with the issue at hand in the first part of the session.

In these situations, a parent may need to assert rules and control to keep child safe. A child may also be testing whether a parent who had neglected, abused, or abandoned a child in the past would be able to maintain safety rules when challenged or whether, a dominant crisis mode will continue, even on days with therapy sessions. Therapists can utilize the goals of *Real Life Heroes* to emphasize safety first and rebuild trust and respect including parents' guiding children to be safe. |
| **Children do not trust adults to believe** them | Often, children will test adults to see if they will allow them to share or believe them. More frightened children will often test adults in covert or even sneaky ways, reflecting their experience that sharing has not been safe. Caring adults need to know that the process of testing is both normal and necessary for a child to find out if it is safe to open up their feelings and beliefs. Children need to find out if adults will criticize them in a shaming manner or become too stressed to deal with real situations and experiences. Testing can be facilitated by allowing young children to dictate stories to adults. Therapists or caring adults can help by carefully writing down exactly what the child says, using the child's words. The child can then see that the adult is truly hearing the child's story and not trying to change it to fit the adult's perspective or wishes. |
| Child **fears recurrence** of traumas | Open up possibilities to prevent any future traumas by asking the child to consider:

How would (child's heroes) have handled this?

What could have made it just a little better?

What could have helped you and (other people in the story)?

Who could help? |

If . . .	Then . . .
Child **wants to work alone** on pages	The life storybook was not designed to be a project for the child to work on by himself or herself; however, some children may prefer to do sections by themselves and then share their work later with their therapist or family members they can trust. The intent in both cases is to safely rebuild positive memories and trust in caring adults as well the child's trust in himself or herself.
The **child balks** when asked to consider possible solutions to problems illustrated in the child's artwork or stories	Work on solutions should not be forced. Rather, a therapist can ask questions like: Was this fair? Who could have helped (parents, aunts, uncles, grandparents, friends, neighbors, police, teachers, doctors, etc.)? Who was responsible? Who could help now? This is similar to the cognitive interweave approaches. Such questions can elicit beliefs by children that they were responsible for abuse, family violence, addictions, etc.
The **child blames himself or herself,** taking on adult responsibilities	Challenge inappropriate beliefs with questions that build on child's sensitivity and caring for others, e.g., Do you know any children (at the age of the child during the incident in the story)? "Would a _____-year-old child, like the child you know, be responsible for what happened? Who in the child's family and community could have helped the child? Therapists can also challenge these beliefs by inviting children to consider what other children and adults would say about a similar situation with similar levels of abuse defined as discipline, e.g., "Would your coach (or best friend's mother) say that an eight-year-old was responsible for being burned with hot water and beaten by her stepfather because she left a mess in the kitchen sink?"
Child or therapist want(s) to **target an important skill** for development to counter trauma patterns	An additional thermometer can be used to monitor work on specific goals or skills. For instance, to assess development of a child's level of trust and attachment to a parent or caring adult, therapists could ask a child to rate: How much of your story does a parent/primary caretaker know? How comfortable would you be if _____ (a potential caring adult) was here right now? How would you be feeling right now if _____ knew the whole story? Or, the added thermometer could be used to monitor a child's ability to replace aggressive reactions to identified triggers with calming and constructive actions by rating, e.g., "How much power did you have today to ask _____ (resource) in your class to take a break and . . . (implement anger safety plan)? To make another thermometer, simply trace one of the thermometers in Chapter 19 or invite the children to make their own.

If . . .	Then . . .
Children appear **anxious outside their homes** or therapy sessions	Check for fears reflecting unspoken traumas. When children have experienced violence or threats outside their homes, they typically need specific safety plans to counter these threats, safety plans they can believe. Photographs and concrete symbols of how people care for a child (caring adults who will protect a child) and reminders of how their world is different now can be helpful in reassuring a child. It often helps children to carry these symbols or laminated photos with them and to have them on display in their bedroom and family living areas.
Child appears too distressed to work on pages of the book and cannot be comforted	Consider using this session to work nonverbally on creating materials, e.g., a drum out of a tin can, designing a personalized bookmark (see Chapter 22), or inventing a musical instrument. Creating materials that foster a sense of safety would be very valuable. That could include arts and crafts projects, e.g., making a shield from cut-out cardboard decorated with symbols representing strengths and powers or making a photo cube with pictures of people the child likes.
Parent or guardian disrupts sessions by screaming at child for past misbehavior, e.g., "You're grounded!"	Therapists need to assert the importance of sessions and the need for boundaries. This is especially important when therapists are working in homes or with nonvoluntary clients. Engagement of parents, guardians, and children requires therapists to be strong, respectful *and* real. One therapist (Brown, 2005) using this model countered a parent's yelling at a child by saying, "Don't mess with my time." This worked because the therapist had established mutual respect over time with both the parent and the child, demonstrating to the parent that the therapist was committed to both of them and understood that discipline was also important.
	No therapy can take place when sessions are used as a time for parents, or anyone else, to berate a child, or when therapists and other caring adults do not keep sessions safe. At the same time, therapists can respect the positive part of a parent's or guardian's efforts to guide or protect a child. Parents and guardians may benefit from help to get a break for themselves and to learn more effective ways to set limits and guide children that avoid repeating the trauma behavior cycle, especially triggers for the child or the adult.
Private space is not possible, either in a clinic or the child's home	Through collaborative links to community agencies, e.g., community systems of care, it may be possible to find a community center, religious institution, boys or girls club, etc., willing to provide a room for weekly sessions. Use of indoor public spaces, such as a fast-food restaurant is difficult due to distractions.

If . . .	Then . . .
Therapists feel anxious or uncomfortable with use of trauma therapy protocols, creative arts or life story work	Therapists can develop comfort in the use of trauma therapy protocols and creative arts modalities by practice in peer consultation and with ongoing supervision in trauma and attachment therapy. Therapists can develop comfort and skills with the use of creative arts as they complete their own workbooks by: picking from a range of colors, sketching an abstract drawing, tapping out notes and experimenting with simple chords, tapping out their chord with their own simple rhythm, then acting it out with the *Action Pose*. Just as with the children, it's helpful take a relaxed, playful attitude and explore creativity. Taking yoga or dance lessons, movement exercises, music lessons, can also be helpful as well as rewarding.
Child becomes distracted when soothing self in response to sounds of other children or family members and resumes threat-avoidant behaviors	Check on reminders and triggers for unresolved safety issues. Work with child to practice daily on building skills in concentration and balance with fun activities, e.g., juggling Nerf balls or balancing peacock feathers with therapist or peers trying to distract child with progressively increasing sounds, words, calls, or movement.
Difficulty **arranging a special space in home-based work**	Establish structure of sessions (Mormile, 2005) beginning with laying out a special sheet or blanket on floor, establishing where everyone will sit, using glockenspiel to sound beginning of session, checking in with thermometers, and moving on with session structure.
Parent wants special time to meet before work begins on workbook	Establish a structure in sessions (Mormile, 2005), with first fifteen minutes to talk with parent followed by session structure.
Child refuses to do one part of sequence, e.g., tapping a rhythm or an Action Pose	Therapists can encourage the child to come up with preferred alternatives. No aspect of this work should be forced. It is important, however, to find ways to help child feel safe and emotionally regulated long enough with each workbook page to reduce the intensity of any traumatic memories. This may mean very little time for many pages but longer for others.

Checkpoints

_____ Therapist establishes a ritualized sequence that works to help the child feel safe and emotionally regulated long enough with each workbook page to reduce the intensity of traumatic memories and to build strong memories of strengths and resources.

_____ Child demonstrates he or she feels safe with therapist by sharing memories, beliefs, and feelings.

_____ Child tests whether therapist will maintain "sanctuary" of sessions by checking on whether safety plans will be implemented.

*PART II:
REAL LIFE HEROES—
CHAPTER BY CHAPTER*

Chapter 1

Affect Power:
Recognizing and Expressing Feelings

Objectives

Begin affect management skill development by helping child to:

- Identify and accept feelings in self as normal body reactions
- Recognize and identify feelings in others
- Calm and center sufficiently to work on tasks
- Maintain self-control
- Express feelings with color, drawings, rhythm, tonality, movement, and words
- Allow child to test "Pledge" of caring adults and begin work on strengthening attachments by sharing work at the end of sessions, or in a special session with safe, caring adults

Overview

The first steps in a journey are often described as the hardest. Therapists play a critical role in inspiring confidence and building momentum as the child "crosses the threshold" into life story work and masters the demons of past traumas. Chapter 1 provides opportunities to build rapport and develop a solid working alliance between therapist and child. Initial activities foster a sense of fun and recognition of a child's strengths while at the same time starting work on affect modulation skills for the quest ahead. Chapter 1 also introduces the child to the structure of sessions and the therapist's role in fostering a safe routine regardless of the crises in the child's world.

Therapists can reduce shame by stressing that feelings are part of what make us human and by helping children to understand that what makes us happy, sad, or angry is important for developing strengths and creating an accurate life story. Later, with safety steps in place, children's work can be shared with caring adults. This can help children discover whether it is safe to share feelings with those adults and inform therapists whether it will be necessary for additional safety work by adults in the children's life, or to begin searching for other committed, caring adults with whom the child can feel safe. Children can also be encouraged to test out safety plans for known traumas and to share concerns that arise so that the therapist and caring adults can develop additional safety plans.

Healing from traumas is facilitated by working with right-brain processes and reciprocal interactions with caring, safe adults. Bolstering skills regarding feeling recognition and different modes of expression are essential for achieving the objectives of later chapters. By practicing these skills, children will become more confident in their ability to recognize their own feelings and develop the security and skills to move beyond a constricted sense of self within relationships with therapists and with safe and caring adults.

Real Life Heroes: Practitioner's Manual
Published by The Haworth Press, Inc., 2007. All rights reserved.
doi:10.1300/5639_07

This work continues, chapter by chapter, as the child moves through the workbook. The goal is to help children develop and practice the skills to recognize triggers, understand how trauma works, and calm themselves, before moving into work on trauma processing in Chapter 8.

Step by Step

Use "Session Summary" (Chapter 21) to establish a consistent order for sessions:

- Self-Monitoring: Knots, Personal Power, Sad, Mad, Glad thermometers
- Safety assurances: Review of signal if child becomes distressed; check by therapist for safety issues
- Ritual opening:
  — Creating a special time/place with herbal tea or snack
  — Focusing/centering exercise (deep breathing, imagery, balancing, etc.)
  — "Magical Moment" (magic tricks)
- Chapter pages:
  — First: nonverbally with drawing, rhythm, tonality, and Action Pose
  — Second: encourage child to create a story with drawing, rhythm, tonality, or movement
  — Third: invitations to respond to questions on workbook page and share stories verbally as a narrative, highlighting strengths and coping strategies
  — Optionally, add dance, photographs, video, or collages
- Repeated self-check: Knots, Personal Power, Sad, Mad, Glad thermometers
- Reassurance: thoughts or feelings to be expected
- Between-sessions work: Practice in self-soothing in different situations and, if possible, additional workbook pages
- Time/date for next session

A peacock feather (Macy, 2004) is very useful to engage children in centering activities at the beginning of sessions. The child can be encouraged to experiment, balancing the feather in different ways: (1) in a balanced position with knees bent, feet comfortably spread, shoulders centered over hips, eyes on the top of the feather with head upright, and deep smooth breathing; (2) legs tensed or body tilted to the side; (3) while saying a negative belief, e.g., "Everybody hates me" or "I'm bad, really bad;" (4) while moving quickly around the room in a hyper manner; or (5) with eyes darting every way watching every corner of the room. Once a child has become comfortable balancing the feather, it is useful to point out lessons or imagery, e.g., how looking at the top keeps our heads centered and we become aware, even without words, when the feather first starts to tilt, and then we can make tiny adjustments, whereas if we focus down on the bottom of the feather, we are only able to see larger changes and then need to make bigger adjustments. This is similar to how developing skills for body scanning and increasing awareness of body reactions helps us to cope better with stressors *before* things get more difficult.

Children can be encouraged to build their feather skills by gently tossing feathers from one hand to another and later by passing feathers to the therapist or a caring adult. Passing the feather could also be used as a signal to move on to the next phase of the session.

After introducing feather balancing, children can be encouraged to show on their glockenspiels how their balancing would sound if put to music. If children are not happy with their balancing, they could show, in tones, how they'd like the balancing music to sound and then make a bridge melody to connect their current balancing with how they would like it to sound.

Alternate centering exercises can be developed to match children's and therapists' skills and interests. Blowing bubbles or yoga exercises, such as the "tree" are useful. For instance, to practice balance and breathing with the tree exercise, have children focus their eyes on something in the distance, take several deep full breaths, let out the tension with each exhale, slowly put the right foot near knee, balance, breathe deeply. When comfortable, slowly raise arms from sides of body to touch above head, maintain balance, remind children it's okay to let foot drop and lift again. Like learning to ride a bike, centering exercises need to be practiced over and over to make them natural and available.

Begin workbook exercises by encouraging children to identify something fun that they like to do, things that they are good at, and sports or games that they enjoy. This helps to enrich positive memories and to demonstrate that the therapist will focus on strengths, rather than problems, as many children expect.

The child's choices for fun activities can be utilized to encourage special times with caring adults every day, whenever possible. Therapists can also use the child's favorites as reinforcements for working in sessions or as a fun way to end sessions. Therapists can encourage caring adults in separate sessions to do special things with the child, e.g., crafts, knitting, origami, paint by number, Legos.

Follow up children's illustrations of fun events with questions about times that they remember doing one of the things that they enjoyed, e.g., winning a game, as well as something that they may not have enjoyed like losing at a game. This begins the process of helping children to see that it is possible to acknowledge and accept both good times and hard times as a normal part of life.

To foster creative expression of feelings for each workbook page:

1. Begin by having the child select a special color to sketch each feeling as a free, spontaneous, and simple image, then accentuate details, e.g., asking the child what the figure reminds him or her of, and then encouraging the child to accentuate those features, or possibly to shape an initial sketch into a living being, a plant, an animal, or a person.

2. Identify tone of voice accompanying this image or encourage child to experiment with different intonations.

3. Tap out a rhythm and intensity to match a feeling (e.g., with magic wand or xylophone mallet).

4. Match tone of voice with a note from the xylophone or keyboard and, if desired, experiment with other notes that blend with the first note thereby creating a chord selected by the child to match a particular feeling or task from the workbook. Later, this can be expanded to include two notes or a three-note chord. Alterations in patterns of the notes within chords can then be utilized to generate simple, short melodies. Repetitions of two or three chords can also be utilized to create a mood or feeling (see Austin, 2002).

5. Demonstrate drawing or feelings with Action Pose and promote bodily awareness of each feeling.

6. Identify feelings expressed with drawings, rhythm, chords, and movement using words, asking how child shows feelings, e.g., with a smile, a frown, a clenched fist, etc.

7. Invite child to continue stories from drawings, music, or Action Pose. For instance, encourage continuation of Action Pose with enactments involving movement or dance utilizing the child's metaphors and imagery. For instance, a sports move can be tied to a feeling; e.g., a "happy" dunk shot in basketball, a "sad" free shot, a "powerful" soccer kick at a goal.

8. Encourage children to add stories about their drawings, music, or movements, where possible, with open-ended questions that enlarge their perspective.

9. Highlight positive beliefs stressing strengths and coping with problems.

Ask children to recognize feelings in others and within themselves. This may be challenging for many traumatized children. It is important to emphasize that feelings are natural and universal. Everyone feels fear, anger, sadness, and happiness at different times. For instance, a child who loses a family member who was murdered may feel an urge to strike back. Feelings are not bad or good. Feelings are not the same as actions that we choose (Cohen et al., 2001).

Utilize the Action Pose to ask children to scan over their bodies and heighten awareness of what they feel from their heads to their toes, when they are afraid, angry, sad, and glad, etc.

Use drawings, rhythm, music, and movement to express different feelings and show children how each feeling helps them. In particular, it is important to discuss with traumatized children how fear helps protect them (Macy et al., 2003). By recognizing how their bodies are signaling an emotion, like fear, children can become aware of early warning signals of danger and then implement safety plans developed with caring adults.

Foster skills in recognizing emotions with role-playing and identification of emotions in feeling charts, from photographs in magazines, or illustrated children's storybooks. Other activities include:

- Ask children to tap a rhythm, add tonality, and try out a gesture, movement, and facial look to match each feeling on the chart. Note: for assessments and to encourage storytelling, it is often helpful to ask children to make up a short story for each feeling shown on a feeling chart (Kagan, L., 2005). Storytelling can be fostered by asking the child to add a beginning, middle, and end. See Materials/Supplies (page 3 to order charts).
- Create collages from cut-out photos or combining clips from movies.
- Photograph or videotape the child or others making faces and acting out different feelings.
- Practice making faces and looking at a mirror (Mullin, 2004).
- Ask children to make a list of all the feelings they can think of in three minutes (Cohen et al., 2001). Then draw these feelings, add rhythm and tone with glockenspiels, and enact them with an Action Pose, a simple gesture, or special look.

Invite children to color back of bookmark (Chapter 22). Bookmark can then be laminated to preserve it.

Review safety of child from child's perspective:

- By sharing completed pages of Chapter 1 with therapists and later with other safe, caring adults, children will often test if they can begin to trust the adult(s) who are helping them. Page by page, children watch for nonverbal cues to see if the therapist and other adults validate how they have been successful and accept children's wide range of feelings, providing guidance where needed but without shaming or showing fear of real feelings, perceptions, or disclosures.
- Children will also assess their current safety by watching carefully how authorities respond to their fears about contact with adults or peers, e.g., are children forced to go to visits when they feel unsafe? Have therapists, law guardians, CPS workers, CASA workers, and judges taken the time to hear a child's story? Have viable safety precautions been implemented that match risks? Are authorities advocating mandates that children return to unsafe homes and relationships as "goals?" Can authorities voice the experiences and fears children carry from past traumas, or do authorities appear to be placating adults who have neglected or abused children, fearful of lawsuits, or unable or unwilling to say out loud in front of the children what has been reported?

Use the "Knots" and "Personal Power" thermometers at the beginning and end of each session to guide a child to step back, self-monitor, and share with therapists how he or she is feeling. It is important to check in with a child periodically throughout a session and the thermometers can be used at any time. This will help the child begin to connect external variables with differences in his or her internal states. Thermometers also provide a means for the therapist to validate a child's ability to stop work that becomes too painful and to remind a child to utilize self-soothing skills.

Pay attention to what a child identifies as triggers to feelings of anger, fear, sadness, and courage.

Pitfalls

- Therapist urges child to reveal or disclose feelings or experiences when child is still living in an unsafe home.
- Therapist is too uncomfortable with expression of feelings, or with creative arts, e.g., music or movement, leading child to feel constricted.

Troubleshooting

If . . .	Then . . .
Child is **reluctant to start**	Accentuate how these sessions are different than other types of relationships a child may have had in the past by encouraging child to utilize nonverbal modalities to illustrate different emotions. Therapists can foster experimentation rather than production by working creatively themselves with modalities they enjoy and by respecting a child's responses rather than evaluating or judging what the child creates.
	Creativity is fostered by emphasizing the process rather than focusing on achieving results.
Child refuses to draw	Ask child to form a picture in his or her mind and hold it there while sharing image with rhythm, tonality, and an action movement. Afterward, ask child to share details from image and record on workbook page. Children can also be invited to use photos, videos, cut-out pictures, or collages.
Child shows a **limited range of responses on thermometers**	Many children initially indicate on their thermometers a narrow band of responses, e.g., three to four, in every situation; or conversely, an all-or-nothing perspective, e.g., marking ones or tens, for every situation. To help children develop a greater ability to sense their own feelings, ask them to tap a rhythm, to vary intensity, and add notes on the glockenspiel to show a low Knots rating, then the highest Knots possible, followed by a Knots level in between.
	Similarly, ask the child to tap out a rhythm with varying intensity, and add notes for low *Personal Power,* the highest possible *Personal Power,* and in between. Children can also be invited to enact these feelings with a gesture, dance step, or safe athletic/gymnastic move. Children can also be asked what would have to happen to lead them to feel just a tenth more or less, then a level they have indicated on a thermometer.
Child has **limited range of feelings**	Hang feelings charts displaying a range of different feelings to foster a sense of acceptance and permission to try out different feelings and to associate visual images with words. It is helpful to practice identification of feelings with visual imagery, rhythm, tonality, facial looks, gestures, and words.

If . . .	Then . . .
Child has **difficulty developing ability** to recognize or express feelings	For many children, this may require practice, as recognition and especially expression of feelings have been severely constricted with traumas or perceived threats. Some children may need extended time to work on developing these skills and can come back to these pages as they continue to work on expanding resources and strengths.
Child **needs additional practice** learning to identify feelings	Games, e.g., Emotional Bingo (Mitlin, 1998), the Mad, Sad, Glad Game (Peak Potential, Inc., 1999), and the Stamp Game (for older children and teens) (Black, 1984), are useful to help children learn to identify feelings.
Child is **action-oriented** and reluctant to draw or write	Encouraging children to act out different emotions or guess different emotions that the therapist acts out may provide a more engaging and active way of exploring different emotions. For other children, it may be helpful to encourage movement or dance. The therapist could be responsible for making notes or recording other salient elements during a session, while the child remains free to use dance or other movements to illustrate feelings.
Child has **difficulty managing multiple tasks**	Limit children to what they can handle, e.g., one or two tasks at a time, and divide up tasks to make them more manageable during sessions. The therapist could be responsible for jotting down the child's narrative responses.
Child has **difficulty or dislikes one or another modality,** e.g., drawing	Providing choices to the child is important to foster means of moving beyond constraints associated with trauma. Accordingly, if a child appears to be having trouble with one form of expression, for example, drawing, it's fine to encourage use of other modalities. Some children may be more comfortable acting out different emotional states, while others may be most comfortable sketching with charcoal or selecting colors from a color wheel or fabrics with different textures to express feelings. The goal is for the child to build strengths with different expressive mediums, to have fun with activities, and, to promote special talents in a particular medium of interest to the child. For disturbing memories, the goal is also to engage the child long enough in safe activities so that anxiety can be reduced before the child moves on to something else.
Child becomes **tense or agitated when asked to share**	The child's behavior often reflects unresolved fears involving a specific adult and the child should not be required to share with that person. The child may prefer to share with other significant parent figures. They can also be encouraged to express their feelings, wishes, and concerns in a safer or more comfortable way through letters, tapes, or in conjoint or subsequent sessions.
	If sharing is unsafe, a child in placement needs to be given a sense of hope that authorities understand the child's predicament and will work to protect a child from being forced to return to unsafe situations or a dangerous home.

If . . .	Then . . .
Child **refuses to draw and share**	If children are unwilling to draw or share in the first chapters, they may be experiencing current threats or believe, based on past experiences and messages (verbal or nonverbal), that they, or people they love, are unsafe. This is especially true if they are worried about identifying or sharing feelings. Careful assessments of a child and family's safety are essential including use of projective tests and play during individual evaluations to check for mandates or messages, often nonverbal, received by child to block expression. A comprehensive attachment and trauma-centered psychological evaluation is usually necessary in order to develop effective interventions and viable safety plans. Evaluations also can uncover the caring and strengths of family members that can, in turn, lead to their involvement in strength-based trauma therapy.
Child has been **threatened** or appears **intimidated**	If a child has been threatened, or appears intimidated, by a family member or another person, the child can be reassured that disclosures in life story work will remain confidential within the limits of the law and ethical practice. Therapists need to acknowledge their responsibilities to bring in authorities if a child was neglected or abused, or if someone is in danger of being harmed. Success in these situations often requires orders of protection, supervision of any contacts with perpetrators, and transfer of custody of the child to someone who can be trusted to protect the child from any threats with monitoring by authorities, e.g., child protective services, and reports to family court.
Child tells therapist to leave, "I want you out of my life!"	Children will often test a therapist's commitment before sharing painful memories such as traumatic events. Therapists have been successful in maintaining engagement by persisting over time. "I'll keep calling." In many situations, therapists can continue working with parents and caring adults while persevering in asking a reluctant child to resume sessions. The key to engaging such children often lies in reducing shame involving the child's attributions of self-blame and fears of distressing parents the child fears losing. Working to help parents and guardians understand how trauma works and their influence in helping the child overcome fears can be useful to engage adults to lead the way for their children, to reassure the child that parents and guardians will be okay, and to insist that the children work on healing and recovery.

Checkpoints

_____ Child identifies and accepts basic feelings in self and others including: anger, fear, sadness, and courage.

_____ Child recognizes feelings in others including kindness and caring, sadness, fear, anger.

_____ Child shares drawings and feelings with therapist and, where possible, with one (or more) safe caring adult(s).

_____ Therapist learns several special interests and strengths of child.

Chapter 2

Finding and Strengthening Heroes

Objectives

Develop child's understanding of heroes by helping child to identify:

- Heroes from media, fantasy, books, popular icons
- Attributes and actions of people acting as heroes that appeal to the child
- How heroes find resources by building self-awareness, self-control, and by getting help from others (allies) in order to restore safety and overcome adversity
- Real people in their lives who act as heroes

Develop child's affect management skills with tie to heroes' abilities and how heroes need to practice skill development

Overview

The image of heroes, male and female, can be utilized to renew children's hope and the courage to continue along a journey of recovery, moving beyond the constraints of their fears. Therapists can often utilize assessments of attachments to tap into a child's unspoken wishes, identify people from the child's past who acted as a child's hero, or to build relationships with new people who could become heroes and help overcome traumas. Imagery of heroes can also ward off feelings of vulnerability and help children feel safe enough to experiment with new solutions.

The meaning of heroism can be introduced by asking the child to draw someone that the child admires. Afterward, discussion may touch on the different traits that a particular individual possesses that make him or her special. For example, if a child is very interested in sports, a sports hero could be identified that the child admires and optimally who is similar to the child in some way, e.g., the child's ethnic heritage or experiences. The child can then be encouraged to learn about what helped this hero succeed, who helped this person, how did she or he develop special skills, and how did she or he overcome adversities. Consider each hero's strengths and weaknesses, how they faced challenges or danger, what helped them stay safe and overcome problems, and how they were able to get help along the way, e.g., from mentors, family members, teachers, coaches, etc.

Real Life Heroes: Practitioner's Manual
Published by The Haworth Press, Inc., 2007. All rights reserved.
doi:10.1300/5639_08

Discussing heroes provides an opportunity to help children learn how ordinary people become heroes. Emphasize how everyone has weaknesses, just like fictional superheroes. Superman was weakened by kryptonite. Luke Skywalker was impulsive. Heroes learn to overcome their weaknesses by being honest with themselves and having the courage to change. Famous heroes can be used to emphasize that courage, like other skills, is learned through repeated practice (Miller, 2002). We can help our children become heroes by encouraging them to practice being brave in safe ways and by asking them to share everyday acts that demonstrate courage.

Discussing heroes also provides a natural link to identifying attributes a child admires. Attributes include skills the hero relies on when going through tough times to remain centered enough to think and plan, and strong enough to heal from wounds including the ability to ask for and accept help from family and friends. The "Superhero Band-Aid" exercise provides a valuable segway to foster self-soothing and affect-management skills. Affect-management skill development includes developing the ability to calm oneself with imagery, music, rhythm, deep breathing, meditation, progressive muscle relaxation, sports, dancing, singing, and writing poetry or journals. This exercise also provides a nice link to introduce cognitive behavioral techniques including self-monitoring (thermometers), thought stopping, refocusing one's sight and thoughts on positive safety factors, and decreasing preoccupation with searching for and detecting perceived risk factors. Self-soothing skill building can then be incorporated into a safety plan for managing feelings of distress from within or without.

This chapter also presents an opportunity to strengthen the therapist's rapport with the child and for the child to become more comfortable exploring different aspects of his or her personality and heritage which make him or her unique.

Step by Step

Help the child identify fictional heroes (from books, movies, TV shows, athletes, artists, and other people in the media) who the child admires. Therapists can draw on autobiographies for children about famous and important people, interviews with prominent athletes, artists, and representatives of different ethnic groups, including the child's own ethnic or cultural group. The "Heroes Library" (Chapter 16) lists recommended books for children about heroes from different ethnic groups for three reading levels. It is highly recommended that each agency or clinic have a Heroes Library matching the ages, reading level, and ethnic heritage of clients.

Invite the child to explore different types of heroes who are fictional as well as real. This exploration should highlight how heroes develop skills over time through practice, how even heroes have fears and weaknesses, and how heroes must work with others to overcome obstacles. Simply put, any heroes without vulnerabilities and weaknesses would be unreal and boring! Even Superman had to watch out for kryptonite. The same is true for Moms and Dads, and boys and girls. Children could be encouraged to take identified heroes and shape them in sketches, in clay, or with musical tones leading to simple stories. Children may wish to create their own storybook, song, or sports move (Action Pose) named in honor of a particular hero.

Ask children to explore the concept of heroes on a more personal level by thinking about different people in their neighborhood, or family and friends who have helped other children. This discussion should highlight the positive beliefs, attitudes, and strengths that these individuals possess.

Highlight heroes' reactions (helpful and unhelpful) to danger and tie this to how boys and girls, men and women have very normal reactions to traumatic events. Emphasize the importance of fostering strengths and avoiding shame by recognizing how everyone has sensitivities and vulnerabilities. Superheroes recognize their weaknesses and work on becoming stronger. This means learning and practice. Reference to popular fictional heroes, e.g., Harry Potter, Luke Skywalker, famous athletes, or singers may be useful.

Before completing Chapter 2, it is important to introduce children to psychoeducational materials that detoxify trauma symptoms and counter the stigma and self-denigration often accompanying traumatic stress. The "survival" alarm bell metaphor (Ford & Russo, 2006) is very useful to teach children and caring adults how traumatic stress and PTSD lead to a bodily state of alarm, an alarm that never seems to end. Chapter 23 provides an introduction to trauma psychoeducation and skill building that is linked to the heroes theme of Chapter 2.

Show children and caring adults how traumatic stress can be viewed as a natural way that our brains protect us when we are threatened with life or death situations, e.g., fears of a beloved sibling dying or parents hurting or killing each other. Staying in hyperalert and alarm mode can become a habitual response that very likely helped at one point in a child's or adult's development. However, being in alarm mode blocks learning, reasoning, and building better relationships. Accordingly, preventing traumatic stress reactions or PTSD means turning down the alarm bells and opening up our abilities to self-soothe, perceive, learn, think, and take charge of our lives (adapted from Ford & Russo, 2006).

The concept of "FREEDOM" (Ford & Russo, 2006) can be used to engage youths to work on building essential skills to prevent or manage stressors including: **F**ocusing, **R**ecognizing child traumatic stress triggers, (accepting) **E**motions, **E**valuating beliefs, **D**efining goals, developing **O**ptions for change, and **M**aking the world a better place. Children should also learn how to calm themselves when they feel stress (their "Knots") by practicing "SOS" (adapted from Ford & Russo, 2006) and included in Chapter 23.

Slow down: One thought at a time; breathe in and out, slower and slower, deeper and deeper, filling up your whole body from the tip of your toes to top of your head . . .

Orient yourself: Focus on right now, in this place; wiggle your toes, listen to your breathing, notice who's around who could help you and look for calming objects you can see or feel . . .

Self check: Slowly scan over your body from the tip of your toes through your feet, ankles, knees, thighs, hips, stomach, chest, arms, and up your neck to your mouth, and all over your head to the very top; rate yourself on My Thermometers (Chapter 19)

To reinforce this, practice an "SOS" ritual: tap in Morse code with child gradually slowing the rhythm. Use glockenspiel or other instruments to practice a note from a chord to match each step: Slow down, orient, self-check, followed by all three notes together.

Encourage children (and caring adults) to practice SOS twice a day along with their own special ways to calm and soothe themselves (e.g., "deep belly breathing"). Also, encourage children to practice SOS in different situations. Continue practicing SOS skills through the next several chapters until child can slow down and self-orient quickly. These skills will be further integrated and reinforced in Chapter 6 as part of the "ABCs of Trauma and the Heroes Challenge."

Introduce child to more advanced self-soothing skills as part of becoming stronger and learning from heroes. Learning self-soothing skills can be compared to learning to ride a bike. Each one may seem awkward or even impossible at first, but with practice, it becomes natural.

First, have the child learn to self soothe in all five senses (after Mahoney, Ford, & Cruz, 2005):

- *Eyes:* Look at a photograph of someone or something that makes you feel peaceful; look at a plants or flowers; find something in every room that makes you feel good inside.
- *Ears:* Listen to relaxing music, or the music in a favorite person's voice, sing along with a "feel good" song.
- *Taste buds:* Treat yourself to a tasty, soothing drink (e.g., hot chocolate or herbal tea), sip slowly and savor.

- *Nose:* Sniff as you sip or pull out your favorite perfume, sniff flowers, a spice, or a favorite treat.
- *Touch:* Smooth a rich peaceful smelling lotion on your hand, take a warm bubble bath, pet a friendly animal, rub a soft piece of fabric.

Second, add movement:

- *Take a walk:* Swim, play a sport, or exercise; learn and practice yoga.

Third, encourage the child to get help from someone the child trusts:

- *Talk to a friend:* Hug someone.

Fourth, have the child write his or her favorite self-soothing activities as part of a safety plan and put the card in his or her wallet, backpack, or pocket along with names and phone numbers of people to call for help:

Safety First

Five Senses Self-Soothing Plan:
   Eyes: _____
   Ears: _____
   Tastebuds: _____
   Nose: _____
   Touch: _____
Action Plan to Relax:

_____
_____

People I can call for help:
   Police: _____
   Teacher/Principal: _____ _____
   Adults I trust: _____ _____
                _____ _____
                _____ _____

   Family Members: _____ _____
                _____ _____

   Friends: _____ _____
                _____ _____

Continue skill development beyond Chapter 23 by teaching children to practice deep breathing, muscle relaxation, imagery, and refocusing skills. Skill training can be linked to developing attributes of admired heroes (e.g., training to become a Jedi knight. Therapists can remind children that practice is one of the secrets behind their heroes skills, just as an athlete, a musician, or an actor practices every day for hours to develop exceptional abilities. Training means practice.

Deep belly breathing begins (Kabat-Zinn, 1990; Cohen et al., 2003, 2006) by instructing children to close their eyes, and then to breathe in so deeply that they feel their bellies rise up and then fall back down as they exhale. Have children count slowly from one to five as they breathe in through their nose, and then exhale through their mouths again counting from one to five. Young children may enjoy watching a small stuffed animal or action figure rise up and down on their bellies as they practice this skill. Deep breathing disrupts children's focus on stressful events by redirecting to the air entering their mouths and strengthening their bodies. Older children can be asked to become aware of any thoughts that come up while practicing belly breathing, but to refocus on breathing and let counting take precedence over competing thoughts. This exercise requires practice and helps children learn to redirect their thoughts while they relax their bodies.

Progressive deep muscle relaxation techniques help children learn to first tense then relax different muscles in their bodies. This usually begins with tensing their toes, holding the tension, counting from one to five, and tying this in with deep belly breathing. This skill requires practice, working up the body from the toes to the arch of the foot, through the calf, thigh, back, upper arms, lower arms and fists, neck, and head.

Music and rhythm can also be used to help a child relax. Many children have favorite songs that help them feel calmer. Remembering and humming a lyric or musical phrase can be used as a signal to help their bodies calm down and refocus attention away from preoccupation with danger signs.

Encouraging a child to develop a detailed image of a safe time and place is also very important. Safe place imagery may be fostered by having children draw a picture of a time when they felt warm, cared for, and secure. Children can be encouraged to add color and accentuate with details the best parts of this picture.

Safe place imagery requires practice to make it useful. Ask the child to redirect thoughts away from whatever is going on to his or her own special safe place. This can be homework exercise along with in-session practice.

As an alternative, especially for children who enjoy music, invite them to use one of their favorite songs, a verse or two that makes them feel upbeat and good about themselves. This can become a "safe song," and again should be practiced in different situations until the child can bring it to mind easily, even when stressed.

With many children, it is helpful to encourage them to create a special memento, e.g., a stone or laminated picture symbolizing the care they remember from a good and safe time in their lives.

Children can be asked to practice diverting a stress-provoking train of thought (thought-stopping) by saying a favorite word or a command, e.g., "Snap out of it!" or utilizing a physical action, such as snapping a rubber band on their wrist (Cohen et al., 2003). Children can then practice substituting relaxing or safe place images and thoughts, e.g., mastering a basketball move, or getting a hug from Grandma, or imagining what will happen next in a book they are reading.

For practice, ask the child to:

- Tense your toes as tight as you can. Then, take a deep breath and tighten up from your toes through your legs, all the way up to your shoulders and forehead, squeezing your eyes (for children who feel safe enough to do so), and holding yourself tighter and tighter.
- Now, empty your head and let the air out as you relax your whole body. Let everything go, every thought, all the tension. Let it all go. Take in a big breath, filling yourself up again. As you breathe in, fill up you mind with pictures and thoughts of your favorite safe and warm places. Or, if you want, fill your mind with your favorite song that makes you feel warm and good inside. You can add your favorite people who make you feel safe and warm. Try to add color and sounds and feelings to the pictures of your safe and warm place.
- Take another deep breath, and try to make the picture and thoughts even stronger. Try to keep your mind focused on that picture.
- Afterward, reinforce the child for taking power away from painful thoughts and taking control of what he or she wants to think about.

Encourage positive attributions and self-direction. It's important to recognize a child's true beliefs and to accentuate the positive aspects of what he or she likes about themselves. This can begin with abilities the child illustrates in Chapter 1 as well as abilities the child demonstrates to cope with stress and past traumas, skills that can be redirected to help a child succeed. Refocusing on positive self-statements, e.g., "I can do this," or "I've done this before" helps a child avoid becoming caught up in reactive behaviors that lead to problems.

Assign homework to practice skill development in a fun way and to use body-awareness skills as a signal to SOS and use other favorite self-soothing strategies. For instance, feelings of tension or noticing how their fist is beginning to clench can be useful as warning signs to indicate when children should slow down and calm down, pull out a momento of a warm memory, or visualize a special person's face smiling. The goal is to make skills as automatic as riding a bike, and to encourage children to develop their favorite ways to relax before fears or anger lead them to become out of control.

Pitfalls

- Rushing through heroes work to focus on problems.
- Presenting heroes as all knowing, all powerful, and perfect, thus creating standards children can never attain.
- Minimizing how heroes develop skills slowly with practice and instruction and how real heroes feel frightened but learn how to utilize their reactions to help them overcome hardships.

Troubleshooting

If . . .	Then . . .
Child appears **hesitant, or too blocked** to develop a hero story with a beginning, middle, and end	Encourage children to make up a heroes comic book featuring their own hero mastering some challenge or, if preferred, develop hero images with puppets, paper maché, clay, etc. Enact stories or compose hero music, rap songs, drum beats. Develop a hero's game including obstacles and resources that are similar to a child's life.
Action-oriented child cannot verbalize how **heroes could help in real life**	Practice "moves" of the child's heroes from sports, theater, movies, etc., to help child see how this feels; then explore through fantasy, and enactments how these "powers" could be used to handle different situations.
Child **does not identify heroic qualities in family or community**	Write out traits a child admires on cards and match these traits to a stack of cards identifying people from a child's life including family members, teachers, coaches, clergy, etc.
Child **lacks understanding of cultural strengths** from her heritage	Visit historical sites commemorating "heroes," especially men and women from the child's ethnic background.
Child **lacks recognition of people in community** helping others	Ask caring adults to take child to visit community organizations to see or interview people making a difference in the lives of people in child's community.

If . . .	Then . . .
	Go online and look up advocacy and service organizations that address areas of interest or concern for child, e.g., animal care, hunger, human rights, safety for women, child abuse, racism, etc.
Child **lacks appreciation for how he or she can help** others	Involve youth in activities that offer opportunities to help others, e.g., mentoring younger children, helping senior citizens' centers, caring for animals in veterinary hospitals and shelters or farms.

Checkpoints

_____ Child identifies heroes from media, fantasy, books, and popular icons.

_____ Child identifies attributes and actions of people acting as heroes that appeal to child.

_____ Child identifies how heroes find resources and work together to create safety and overcome adversity.

_____ Child identifies real people in his or her life who act as heroes.

_____ Child develops "Safety First" plan card including who to call for help and use of SOS.

_____ Child practices basic self-soothing skills including: deep belly breathing, progressive muscle relaxation, safe place imagery, and thought-stopping.

Chapter 3

Caring Adults from the Past:
Mentors and Guardians for the Future

Objectives

- Strengthen child's positive memories of caring adults and how they helped child in the past.
- Identify at least three important people and possibilities for reconnecting including people who cared for the child in the past and people who child would like to count on now or in the future.
- Enlist, wherever possible, caring adults to help child learn from the past and develop strengths for the future.

Overview

Chapter 3 renews and expands memories of people who cared for a child. Children who have suffered through traumatic events often lack the resources to remember both positive and negative events without becoming distressed. Working with a child in the safe environment of a therapeutic relationship can help a child to recall and strengthen positive memories, especially the images and affects associated with family members and other important people who affirmed the child's importance and value.

As in Chapter 3, caring adults serve as mentors and guides in children's quest to rebuild a positive view of their lives. Children often respond well when the therapist and caring adults work with the child as detectives. Activities can be presented as detective work to recover positive events and especially positive acts of caring. The therapist can use activities to elicit support from adults in the child's life to help a child rediscover strengths from the past and resources for the future.

Step by Step

Identify people who can help a child learn about what happened in the past, identify strengths, and open up possibilities for future positive relationships.

Highlight people who cared for the child when the child was hurt or sick.

Accentuate details of positive memories: smells of cooking, the taste of Grandma's fried chicken, the look on a caretaker's face, the warmth of a safe place. These activities can provide openings to strengthen a child's self-soothing abilities.

Along with drawing a safe place, encourage child to try out and then practice a rhythm and tones to reinforce this image. Ask the child to look at the safe place drawing, then tap out a rhythm that matches the picture. Next, pick one to four notes on the glockenspiel to go along with the picture and tap the rhythm on those notes. Similarly, repeat this process for a rhythm

Real Life Heroes: Practitioner's Manual
Published by The Haworth Press, Inc., 2007. All rights reserved.
doi:10.1300/5639_09

and notes to match both the highest Personal Power level on the thermometer and the lowest Knots.

These notes, chords, and rhythm patterns can then be practiced along with imagery of a safe place, and used as reminders to help children calm their minds and bodies, and to remind them of soothing and powerful music that can drive away noise or anxiety-provoking perceptions.

Engage relatives and service providers to provide information by:

- asking for their help to help the child;
- showing respect for what they have done and their special roles;
- sharing questions in advance;
- asking them to signal if questions become too difficult or upsetting;
- indicating that therapist will stop questions whenever asked to do so.

Remind extended family members that you realize if the child is hurting then other caring adults are also hurting. To reduce anxiety over being asked personal questions, it helps to introduce by saying, "I'm a (psychologist, social worker, etc.) and as you probably expect, I tend to ask a lot of nosy questions. I'm going to count on you to tell me if I'm getting too nosy" (Schlosberg, S. in Kagan & Schlosberg, 1989).

Encourage child to learn how famous people or characters were helped by relatives, mentors, or friends to develop special skills, to muster the courage to face adversity, to grieve losses, and to endure hardships; use readings from the Heroes Library (Chapter 16).

When goals are rebuilding or building attachments, gradually include safe caring adults in work during sessions. Amount of shared work should be based on comfort of child and ability of caring adults to foster creativity and spontaneity of child.

When caring adults have met safety criteria, conjoint work can begin by having children share their work on Chapters 1 and 2 with caring adults and have caring adults share their own work on these chapters or similar materials. Typically, children work first alone with therapists and then share with caring adults at the end of sessions.

Next, involve caring adults in work to gather information for the workbook and to answer other questions children may have.

Include caring adults in work on understanding and normalizing how trauma affects children and adults.

Encourage caring adults to explicitly acknowledge how it is normal for child to have both positive and negative memories, beliefs, and feelings about key people and events, including the caring adult or family members with whom the caring adult has had conflict-ridden relationships.

Encourage caring adults to share stories of family members overcoming hardships and to point out skills and family, religious, and cultural values that helped family members succeed.

Encourage caring adults to utilize steps for promoting creativity with children including use of keyboard or other instruments to mirror and harmonize with children.

Encourage use of art, music and *action poses* to express losses and grief shared by child. Therapist and caring adult can validate child nonverbally by matching tones, literally showing that the child is heard, as well as with verbal validation of lost people, time, etc.

Pitfalls

- Inadvertent messages to child that reinforce expectations that parents, guardians, or other important adults are either all good or all bad; lack of validation for how parents and caretakers may have been both caring and neglectful, abusive, or abandoning at different and often unpredictable times.

- Lack of respect, validation, or detective work to help child recover the caring parts of parents and other caretakers who may have been abusive or neglectful at times, e.g., when intoxicated or when triggered into their own traumatic stress responses.

Troubleshooting

If . . .	Then . . .
Child **lacks memories of three caring adults**	Think broadly over time and use fantasy exercises, check past records, and ask to look at photo albums and other family records. Identify past therapists, collateral support, and caring adults who could be involved to help child search for lost extended family, mentors, coaches, teachers, employers, and clergy. Utilize *Attachment Ecogram* (Chapter 17), *Important People* survey (Appendix D) from assessments, and projective testing, e.g., family figure play, the *Roberts Apperception Test* (Roberts, 1986) to help identify images of past caretakers.
Caring adults appear reluctant or resistant to help	Check for misunderstanding of purpose of life story work and offer to meet with prospective caring adults to share information on *Real Life Heroes* including workbook. Emphasize importance of child understanding strengths in family. See also guidelines for engaging family members and service providers from *Families in Perpetual Crisis* (Kagan and Schlosberg, 1989).
Therapist and child are **unable to find three safe caring adults within extended family**	Promote safe, positive, and long-term connections with mentors, coaches, Big Brothers/Sisters, clergy, staff from outreach centers, volunteers from the organizations related to the child's religion, social service organizations, foster families, etc.
Child **lacks** understanding or appreciation of **cultural strengths**	Promote pride in heritage of child's family including race, ethnicity, and celebrations of culture with visits to historical sites, exploring music, food, magazines, and books, contacting community leaders, and visiting relatives with a strong positive cultural identity.
Family members are not able or willing to help child	Provide help to child in grieving losses of adults who are not able or willing to care for child. Differentiate grief over lost love, commitment, and caring from child's loyalty to family members and respect for family members, especially elders, as part of child's culture and upbringing. The child can still respect a family member while at the same time grieving the loss of what child hoped for from that family member. Normalize grief reactions, seek validation from caring family members of appropriateness of grieving lost love and caring, develop grief rituals with family members if possible, and help children to see how significant people in their families, cultures, and heroes from sports, arts, etc., have become stronger over time by facing hardships and developing strengths to persevere.

If . . .	Then . . .
Parents and children remind each other of past traumas	Before involving family members and children together in sessions, it is important that intrafamilial triggers to trauma reactions are identified and diffused, wherever possible. These include environments, e.g., a grandparent's home where abuse occurred, emotional feelings, and anniversary dates. Safety plans need to be developed and practiced for each family member who has upset the child. This is especially important when parents and children remind each other of people who hurt them in the past. This can include parents' memories of traumas around the age or same sex as child, or victimization as a child by another child who looked like or was the same age of the parents' own child at this time. A child may also remind a parent of a violent spouse, especially if the child is of the same sex or develops some of the same facial or behavioral responses. At the same time, nonoffending parents may remind a child of past traumas that the parent did not prevent, and of course, parents who have hurt a child in the past, emotionally, physically, or sexually, will trigger a child's traumatic responses. In each case, a look, a gesture, or an intonation may be enough to trigger a traumatic response.
Parents or guardians provide material support but appear **unable to validate child's experiences** or talk about "family business"	Adults who are committed to providing physical or financial support but cannot validate a child may be willing to help by preparing materials for sessions, e.g., photo albums, birth certificates, immigration documents, special markers or colored pencils. Encourage parents and guardians to share positive stories of strength as a way of teaching values and important life skills. Simply giving permission out loud for a child to go and work with a therapist on life story materials represents a positive message. When possible these adults can be encouraged to work on personal obstacles in therapy, or, to bring in supportive family elders or clergy who would support parents and guardians validating children's experiences. Other relatives or caring adults may be engaged to help a child with skill building or sharing family stories of overcoming hard times.
Child and parent/guardian are too uncomfortable to work together	If a parent/guardian or a child are too uncomfortable to work together on sharing their experiences, it may be helpful to bring in a trusted relative or a friend who can serve as a caring adult (see Caring Adult section). The caring adult may make it possible for a child and a parent to feel safer together.
Family members and caring adults are **living at distant locations**	Arrange telephone calls, e-mail, or, if possible, travel to get "the facts," with safety precautions, "protectors" accompanying child.

Checkpoints

_____ Child becomes able to recall how three people helped child in the past, even in small ways.

_____ Child becomes able to identify at least three current or potential caring adults including adults who cared for the child in the past and adults whom child would like to count on now or in the future.

Chapter 4

Good Times: Bonding
with Allies and Mentors

Objectives

- Help child to recover positive memories of having fun and succeeding that were obscured by traumas.
- Help children and caring adults to share positive memories reinforcing strengths and relationships.

Overview

Chapter 4 helps children recall positive events in their lives and utilize these events to shape positive beliefs about their competence and identity. This chapter can be used to enhance children's pride in their accomplishments and to tie this to how they would like to make their world better, for instance, with a campaign slogan if they were was running for president. These activities promote a sense of the child's life as a quest, in which the child can help others, and at the same time, build a positive identity, rather then remain feeling stuck as "damaged," a "victim," or as unforgivably "bad."

Remembering some of the child's best times also provides vital clues for identifying people who helped in the past and who could possibly help in the future. Rebuilding connections with allies and mentors is crucial in order to grieve losses and overcome hardships. Chapter 4 renews a child's hope for connections, for example, by imagining the power to create his or her own special "holiday" (adapted from Evans, 1986) and other activities that accentuate relationships with important people. The "good times" of the past foster confidence and camaraderie that will help a child have good times in the future.

Step by Step

Engage child to share interests and activities child enjoys, including who the child enjoys playing with and learning from now and in the past. Help child to add details to memories of success including what helped child succeed and child's beliefs about skills and talents.

Engage child to recall and share memories of times when the child felt good, even in small ways, with others. Help child to add details including who else was there, what their faces looked like, what they did, what the child did, how did child feel. . . .

If needed, continue detective work from earlier chapters to build up child's record of "good times." Arrange safe interviews with caring adults in extended family and community, record interviews, develop a visual record of child's past successes with drawings, photographs, or video, and help child obtain concrete symbols of past successes and good times such as trophies or photographs of child holding fish caught, batting, at a family party, etc.

Real Life Heroes: Practitioner's Manual
Published by The Haworth Press, Inc., 2007. All rights reserved.
doi:10.1300/5639_10

Accentuate images and memories of child with caring adults highlighting positive beliefs about child.

Pitfalls

- Leaving child with belief or expectation that good times are free of problems or that a lack of positive memories means that the child is "damaged," "weak," or "bad."
- Leaving child with beliefs that skills and successes are expected without mentoring, coaching, practice, and opportunities to learn while making mistakes.

Troubleshooting

If . . .	Then . . .
Positive memories lead repeatedly to **loops of negative memories** and increasing distress	Help child learn to use self-soothing skills, SOS (Slow down, Orient, Self-check; Ford & Russo, 2006) and "thought-stopping" (see Chapter 2 for detailed guidelines). Practice watching for signs of stress, scanning from the tips of toes to the top of child's head, then utilizing child's favorite self-soothing activity and SOS. Remind child of the difference between normal stress and severe stress, using "Traumatic Stress and the Hero's Challenge" handouts introduced in Chapter 2. Emphasize how tough times can overpower good memories including memories of people who cared at special times for the child. Encourage the child to accept positive memories and grow these stronger than the tough times.
Child's favorite activities are **immature for age** causing discomfort for caring adults or other service providers	Help caring adults to recognize how traumas impair development and how child can be helped to grow by developing skills and positive beliefs and by overcoming fears associated with traumas.

Checkpoints

_____ Child is able to share positive memories with therapist and, when possible, with safe, caring adults.

_____ Child is able to share two or more positive attributes about self and two or more memories of how child succeeded in the past including how relationships helped foster success.

Chapter 5

Developing the Hero Inside

Objectives

Strengthen children's skills to modulate affective responses and effectively cope with common situations encountered at school, at home, and in the neighborhood.

Overview

Recovery from chronic and severe traumas requires reprocessing the demons, fears, and reaction patterns that have plagued children and families, sometimes for generations. Reexperiencing past traumas for short intervals may strengthen traumatic stress reactions. Establishing safety, building trust, and developing skills need to come first so that tough times from the past can be reexperienced long enough to allow reduction in trauma reactions and desensitization to triggers. Building skills, support, and self-confidence help prevent rekindling or strengthening trauma reactions.

Chapter 5 provides activities to build up children's skills and courage. The chapter begins with the fun of magic tricks to highlight the power of the magician and then invites children to develop their personal powers, as they learn the tricks behind the "magic" of self-control and courage. By using the image of the magician, therapists can engage children to practice and reinforce self-soothing skills that will be necessary for more difficult work ahead. The goal of Chapter 5 is to augment each child's *Personal Power* so the child can master the challenge of facing *tough times*.

This chapter includes work on safe place imagery. Accentuate the key factors in children's art, music, or movement that promote feelings of peace, the ability to concentrate, and positive beliefs about the children's skills and abilities to contribute and succeed at home, at school, or in activities, e.g., sports or music. These can then be practiced and reinforced so that the child can remember, visualize, touch, or enact whatever method helps them. Safe place imagery can be enhanced by tying it to concrete symbols children can carry with them, e.g., laminated photos of people who cared about them, necklaces from important people, a polished stone given to the child by a favorite uncle, the favorite scent of a beloved guardian, etc.

Also, in Chapter 5, children are invited to consider how they would make changes in their lives: today, in the past, and in the future. This helps children develop new possibilities and a positive perspective on time that is often lost after chronic and severe traumas.

Chapter 5 ends with a brief self-rating of how each child is managing stress. This can be combined with the Knots and Personal Power thermometers and other measures to indicate whether the child is able to work on changing beliefs in Chapter 6 and reintegrating more painful memories in Chapters 7 and 8. If a child is not ready, additional work is often needed to foster a child's trust in caring adults including taking time to search for and engage adults willing and able to commit to supporting and guiding the child. Children may also need more practice in developing skills, or they can observe how other children and adults have confronted their tough times

Real Life Heroes: Practitioner's Manual
Published by The Haworth Press, Inc., 2007. All rights reserved.
doi:10.1300/5639_11

and became stronger. The self-rating can be repeated after completion of Chapter 6 to see if work on the link between thoughts, feelings, and behaviors reduces the child's distress sufficiently to move ahead with Chapters 7 and 8.

Therapists can build a child's confidence by maintaining the expectation that the child will move through the remainder of the workbook with additional work and support, just as real heroes in real life, move forward, step by step, in their quests to make things better. As in all quests, timing and preparation are important. The therapist's responsibilities are to respect a child's readiness, assess the viability of safety plans, and monitor the progress of caring adults in rebuilding or building trust after traumas.

A checklist is provided in Chapter 25 to help therapists assess whether a child has developed necessary skills and resources and to identify areas where further work is needed. If more work is needed before moving on to Chapter 8, therapists can keep the child moving forward with further development of coping and creative arts skills, as well as efforts to find and strengthen relationships with caring adults.

Step by Step

Enhance skills and resources by imagining "powers" through magic using basic card tricks or other tricks that match the child's developmental level. Encourage child to learn new tricks and take pride in sharing them. Use the metaphor of magic to expand possibilities for figuring out difficult situations that seem, on the surface, to be impossible to solve. Learning how the magician hides the trick reinforces the child's ability to figure out solutions.

Challenge children to connect nine dots with four consecutive straight lines, not lifting their pencils. The Nine Dot Puzzle has been used to encourage children to "break out of the box" to overcome obstacles (see Figure 5.1).

Then introduce the T Puzzle to reinforce looking at puzzles, or tough situations from different perspectives in order to find solutions. Draw a large T about two inches wide, cutting it into different pieces (see Figure 5.2), and ask children to reassemble the "T." Using puzzles also provides opportunities to practice skills in using calming, centering, and "SOS" skills to manage frustration and increase perseverance.

Remember and accentuate times when the child felt safe, highlighting what helped, who was there, and what the child did. Invite the child to share a detailed story of a time the child felt safe by expressing personal interest (after Deblinger, 2005); for instance, "I'd like know more about

FIGURE 5.1. The Nine Dot Puzzle. Instructions: Connect all dots with four connecting lines.

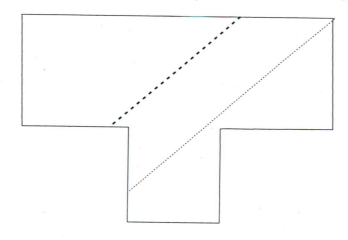

FIGURE 5.2. T Puzzle

that. . . What happened next? What happened right before? . . . Then what happened?" It is also helpful to use body image questions to strengthen a child's recognition of feelings as a means of fostering incorporation of positive beliefs and skills from a positive event, e.g., "If you scanned over your body from your toes to your belly to your head, what were you feeling? What was your heart doing? Your stomach?"

Highlight what the child can do now to feel better. Describe how mastering the calming and self-soothing skills, which the child's real and fictional heroes use to succeed, is similar to mastering sports skills. For instance, learning to swim or ride a bike is difficult at first, but over time with practice and with a few tips, these become easy. Emphasize how the child is training his or her brain and body, just like a professional athlete trains his or her brain and body.

Practice self-soothing skills introduced in Chapter 2 including body relaxation, deep breathing, safe place imagery, a safe song, refocusing attention, chanting, playing music, use of symbols and photos of caring adults, and other concrete actions to reduce stress (see also Fisher, Abarquez, Kitowski, & Sims, 2005). Stress that reducing Knots means taking Action.

Check children's current level of stress and abilities to manage feeling upset with questions and self-rating scale.

Review "Resource Checklist" in Chapter 25 for essential skills and resources and work on developing as necessary. These skills and resources provide a foundation for helping children detoxify past traumas and facilitate success in reintegrating tough times in Chapter 8.

Pitfalls

- Rushing through Chapter 5 without sufficient practice on self-soothing skills or development of sufficient support from caring adults to confront tough times.
- Children may interpret nonverbal messages from therapists or caretakers as a message that they are afraid to deal with child's real life experiences.

Troubleshooting

If . . .	Then . . .
Children are **not able to sufficiently manage affective responses** in order to think about difficult situations without becoming dysregulated	Continue work on developing affect management skills until child can work on materials and stay below a "3" on the "0-5 scale at the end of Chapter 5. Utilize activities amenable to child including: breathing exercises with imagery individualized for child; deep muscle relaxation with changes in environment including lighting, scents, background music; refocusing on comforting stimuli identified in every setting; use of 'time-out' spaces in different situations that child can utilize; developing and practicing safe place imagery including sounds, smells, and scenes; practice songs as meditation; develop sequencing and tonal range with simple musical instruments; try out gestures and develop into movements and simple action movements or dances. Review Chapter 2 guidelines for building affect management skills. Refer, if necessary, to individualized anger management therapy as part of trauma therapy.
Children **lack self-control** abilities	Enroll child in programs that foster self-control and confidence, such as: karate, dance, Project Adventure' programs, and theater arts.
Children appear **too frightened to deal with past traumas**	Enhance or create comforting objects associated with protective and caring adults, e.g., photos, jewelry, special stones, tiny flashlights, perfume, soft fuzzy stuffed animals, etc.
	Add comforting music to meditation and imagery skills and help child practice bringing up soothing tones by memory to counter stress.

Checkpoints

_____ Therapists, caring adults, and children have practiced *and* tested viability of safety plans for children, caring adults, and therapists.

_____ Children and caring adults utilize coping skills to manage frustrations and modulate anger and fear sufficiently to avoid harm to self or others.

Chapter 6

The ABCs of Trauma
and the Hero's Challenge

Objectives

- Ensure that children understand the linkage between thoughts, feelings, and behaviors, how trauma leads to negative thoughts, fear, anger, and failures, and conversely, how positive beliefs, self-awareness, and calming/centering skills lead to success.
- Strengthen and increase children's positive beliefs about their abilities to make things better for themselves and other people.
- Decrease power of dysfunctional beliefs tied to traumas.

Overview

The ABCs of Trauma are introduced to integrate the child's understanding of how trauma affects thoughts, behaviors, and feelings, building on the introduction to traumatic stress in Chapters 2 and 25. This activity helps children understand how trauma can lead to "catastrophic thinking" and failures. Conversely, children learn and practice how they can utilize an understanding of the ABCs to increase the power of their thinking skills and switch to "courageous thinking" to avoid being TRAPPED (Ford & Russo, 2006) in a state of alarm. Children are encouraged to use their full brain instead of just their self-defense reactions as a means of pulling themselves out of trauma reactions and winning their FREEDOM (Ford & Russo, 2006).

The ABCs of Trauma provide a structured exercise to integrate children's skills of centering, increased capacity to focus, and use of positive beliefs in order to better manage low-level stressors. Triggers are identified as well as children's bodily reactions, feelings, beliefs, and behaviors. Children are asked to evaluate what they really want (goals) and to change beliefs and open up new strategies (options) for succeeding.

Chapter 6 focuses on building increased self-esteem and preparing children to successfully decrease the power of their tough times. After completing The ABCs of Trauma, children are invited to continue working on the "hero's challenge" by moving ahead through Chapters 7 and 8 of the workbook. This is a repetition of the Hero's Challenge introduced in Chapter 2.

Step by Step

Complete "The ABCs of Trauma" and the "Hero's Challenge" (Chapter 24). Make sure children understand the connection between thoughts, feelings, and behaviors and how we can be triggered into "fight or flight" modes, losing the capacity to think and figure out how to succeed.

Help children understand that triggers are reminders of things that happened before. In the past, the child may have jumped into an alarm state and fought or run away to survive. Now, the child is older, wiser, bigger, and can get help. Children can respond to triggers with centering,

Real Life Heroes: Practitioner's Manual
Published by The Haworth Press, Inc., 2007. All rights reserved.
doi:10.1300/5639_12

calming, deep breathing, and thoughts about how they can now manage what seemed so horrible at a younger age.

Watch for dysfunctional beliefs and help children overcome self-blame for parent/guardian neglect or abuse while learning to take more control of how their own thinking, which can lead to success and avoid repeated failures.

When possible, encourage the child to share worksheets with safe caring adults. Prepare adults in advance by asking them to complete the ABCs themselves and to become aware of how this process works in their own lives. Then, ask adults to:

- show children that they understand how tough times have led to the child's reactions;
- validate that the adult can understand what led a child to act in a certain way, i.e., the "ABCs of Trauma for that child;
- support how the child is using the power of the child's own thinking to succeed; and
- help the child grow "stronger and stronger" (see Chapter 20).

Encourage caring adults to share memories of good times and bad times as normal parts of their lives, stressing how they, other family members, and heroes from their ethnic group and community have faced and overcome hard times. Ensure that work is tailored to respect the child's cultural heritage.

Check child's Personal Power and Knots thermometers after completion of Chapter 6. Child's Personal Power should be higher than child's Knots before moving ahead to Chapter 8. If not, take time to expand work on increasing self-soothing and self-control skills and replacing dysfunctional beliefs. Chapter 7 can help identify dysfunctional beliefs about past moves that are distressing the child.

Pitfalls

- Using words and activities that don't match child's developmental level.
- Failure to emphasize how taking steps to change behaviors leads to changes in feelings and thoughts about oneself (changing the story of one's life).
- Failure to learn about and respect the child's cultural heritage.

Troubleshooting

If . . .	Then . . .
Children appear **frightened** and lack support from caring adults	Anxious or avoidant children may be responding to fears they experienced in the past or present from guardians or other adults. It is important to check safety plans for the child's home, school, and community. Caring adults can foster courage in children and provide more authentic validation after they have developed their own understanding of what happened in their lives and strengthened their own coping skills. Caring adults should complete complete Chapters 5 and 6 and be able to show mastery of the ABCs of their own lives.
Children **lack sense of past, present, or future**	Reading and discussing books such as Dr. Seuss' *Oh the Places You'll Go!* and *My Many Colored Days* is helpful to normalize experiences of good times and bad times.

If . . .	Then . . .
Children **continue hypervigilant** behaviors	Highlight differences in child's world by encouraging child to dramatize, draw, or write out messages and actions done by important adults "before" as compared to the present time (Sutton, 2004).
Children blame themselves for parents' or guardians' failures, neglect, abuse, drug use, or violence	Often, traumatized children blame themselves for violence or accidents. Blaming themselves provides a sense of control but, at the price of shame and self-denigration. Therapists should watch for negative attributions, e.g., a child blaming herself or himself for a fight between Mom and Dad. It helps to point out that this is a belief that the child developed, very likely, in the middle of a tough time, for instance, the parents' fight. A belief may be right or wrong. Would they blame another child for a similar fight? Did they really have the power, at the age they were, to make Dad hit Mom or Mom stab Dad?
Children bring up **specific problems leading to distress**	Play out possibilities to solve problems child brings up using puppets, family dolls, or through role-plays utilizing understanding and skills from the ABCs of Trauma.
Child demonstrates **anger-control problems**	Utilize activities from *A Volcano in my Tummy* (Whitehouse & Pudney, 1996). Draw what makes child feel angry, how the child's anger would look, and what force would be strong enough to calm the child's anger. For anger problems, help child draw or play out how the child's anger affects others and what happens afterward, (consequences), Help child learn to recognize the first signs of rising anger and then practice implementing self-soothing and redirecting steps in sessions, and later in the child's home, school, and community.
Child needs more practice to understand linkage between thoughts, feelings, and behaviors	Use cognitive behavioral therapy games outlined in Appendix G of *Rebuilding Attachments with Traumatized Children* (Kagan, 2004b) and see TARGET materials (Ford & Russo, 2006) (www.ptsdfreedom.org).
Therapists or caring adults do not feel strong enough to move ahead through *tough times*	Self-care and support is essential for caring adults and therapists, just as for children. Just as airlines tell adults to "put on their oxygen masks" first, caring adults can best help children by developing their own skills for self-soothing, developing supportive relationships, and completing their own life storybooks (see Guardians and Mentors, pages 11-12).

Checkpoints

_____ Children and caring adults can list five positive beliefs about themselves.

_____ Children and caring adults accept responsibility for their own behavior and avoid blaming themselves for the actions of others.

_____ Children demonstrate how they can change behaviors and thus change how they feel and think about themselves.

Chapter 7

Time Lines and Moves

Objectives

Develop a coherent and organized record of child's life by helping child to:

* record factual information about places lived and important people;
* organize important events in child's life in a sequential, time-based order; and
* add meaning to events by including child's ratings of good and tough times.

Strengthen understanding of the universal impact of trauma and how people can grieve losses and grow stronger.

Facilitate child's acknowledgement and expression of losses with validation by therapist, and, when possible, by caring adults.

Overview

Children know that journeys have a starting point and a destination that can be pictured on a map and maps have a magical quality. Maps can lead to buried treasures. Maps can also keep you from getting lost and far away from dangers.

Life story work can be utilized like a map to guide children in their quest to rebuild, or build, attachments to important people. In Chapter 7, children and therapists develop a map that identifies primary resources for the child, key people who have helped the child in the past and who could help the child in the future. In this way, life story work can be seen as a search for buried treasures; like all adventures, children know that dangers exist and many obstacles have to be overcome to reach the treasure.

Real Life Heroes: Practitioner's Manual
Published by The Haworth Press, Inc., 2007. All rights reserved.
doi:10.1300/5639_13

Therapists guide the child along the journey building on the therapist's understanding of how to use resources and confidence that there is a way out of the nightmares of trauma. However, the child and child's family have the information needed to develop the map, including the lessons and experiences to identify both resources and risks that can help or hinder the journey ahead.

This chapter helps children develop a fact-centered record of their lives, including important people and places where they have lived. Traumatized children often feel alone or cast off especially following repeated and severe experiences of violence, loss, or abandonment. Helping children remember people who have helped, even in small ways, can highlight resources, strengths, and talents within themselves, family members, and important people in their lives. Recording facts and identifying these people also helps to diffuse self-blame and accentuate the responsibility of adults to care for and protect children.

Chapter 7 begins work on a child's more difficult experiences including losses. In this work, it is important to acknowledge that the child very likely had both positive and negative experiences with different caretakers, including significant family members. This naturally led to both positive and negative memories, beliefs, and emotional reactions to reminders of those people or situations. By helping children recall people and places in their lives—both positive and negative, therapists, and whenever possible, caring adults, validate children's experiences and, at the same time, demonstrate that it is safe to use creative arts or words to share what happened. This, in turn, provides opportunities for reinforcing good times and reworking negative experiences.

Healing is fostered by promoting acceptance and permission from significant adults in a child's life to hold both the good and the bad. To do this, a child needs the security of caring, protective adults who are strong enough in their own lives to accept that a child may have different, and at times very painful, feelings and memories that adults may wish to forget or ignore. Validation of losses is a key part of work on rebuilding attachments.

Caring adults make significant contributions to a child's recovery by showing a child that it is safe and healthy to learn about both good times and bad times in the past, and to use this understanding to make a better future. By giving children permission to learn about the facts of the past and to share their own memories and feelings, caring adults begin to bridge the gaps that have formed as a result of traumas. Acknowledgement and acceptance of a child's experiences and perspective, including losses and both positive and negative memories is also essential in order for caring adults to attune, or rebuild attunement, with a child.

The questions in Chapter 7 provide opportunities for children and therapists to engage caring adults to help them recover their past by finding relatives and family friends who are able to help children learn what happened especially during the earliest years. By making parts of Chapter 7 a shared activity with a safe parent, relative, or committed adult, children learn that they are not alone and that important people in their lives can see the importance of caring for each other through good and *tough* times. Adults and children can learn from each other what has helped and the skills and courage that helps real people become heroes.

Chapter 7 fosters an understanding of important family members, foster parents, and other people who the child may have had difficulty talking about in previous chapters. This can lead to focused work on rebuilding lost positive connections or grieving losses for the child. Inviting the child's beliefs about the reasons for moves also helps identify self-blame, shame, and feelings of failure and provides opportunities for therapists to help the child replace anger and guilt with more effective coping responses.

Step by Step

Work with children on recording facts, such as dates and places, as a means of recording key events *without* needing to verbalize painful feelings. If this is difficult for the child to do alone with a therapist, it may be necessary to solicit help from caring adults or to return to this section after further work on building safety and self-regulating skills.

Tell the child that caring adults and other therapists or authorities can help to answer questions. The child is not expected to know what happened. It's okay to keep going back to Chapter 7 over the course of work on the life storybook, filling in missing sessions as information becomes available.

Engage child to work as a detective *with* safe caring adults, extended family, libraries, media, hospital records, child protective services, and other community resources to discover what family members and other significant adults did or did not do, what was known, and what interventions were attempted to help a family. Recording of facts is especially important for diffusing self-blame and acknowledging the responsibility of adults to care for and protect children.

If possible, involve caring adults in portions of sessions as sources of information. It is important that caring adults meet safety criteria before involving a child and adult together in activities. Children should not be asked to approach an adult alone unless that adult has validated a child and supported healing including resolving pain from the past as well as the present. Reinforcement of safety rules for sessions and practicing asking questions to these adults may be necessary to reduce a child's anxiety. If adults in a child's family are not safe, the therapist may be able to get information privately from adults by asking for their help or to approach other extended family members and learn about the unsafe adults through multiple sources.

Facilitate expression of feelings by encouraging the child to add color, musical tones or an Action Pose to nonverbally express facts and then afterward, elicit the child's words about what happened. For instance, on the "Life Event" chart, have the child select different colors to reflect feelings (after O'Conner, 1983), and color in the boxes on the left column for each year. Moving horizontally, the child can then elaborate on what happened and use the numeric scale to rate his or her life that year.

Use time lines and other assignments to highlight positive memories and to foster hope for making things better again. Point out how feeling states change for all of us over time by turning time line horizontally. Connect the ratings in the right column to create a graph. Turn the time line chart horizontally and highlight upswings in child's life noting how these upswings related to important people and events. (Note: Adding additional years may be necessary for older children.)

Use Chapter 7 to trace lost relationships and open up possibilities for rebuilding connections wherever possible. Help child to grieve lost relationships and to work on building new relationships.

Identify missing information including questions about a why a child had to move but leave sensitive work for later as child develops trust in therapists and caring adults.

Help child grieve losses shared in the course of storytelling. Mourning losses is a critical part of trauma therapy. Use the following to facilitate grief work (Cohen et al., 2001).

- Identify special parts of past relationships that can't be reclaimed; lost future—what might have been.
- Identify special parts that can be kept alive:
  — How could events (holidays, achievements) be made special even without the lost person, e.g., dedicate award to lost person and what child learned from that person?
  — Include lost person's favorite pastimes, clothes, funniest habit, nicest thing done for child, favorite gift to child, best time child and lost person had together; then use memory books dedicated to lost person.
  — Honor special gifts from lost person in a memorial service including child's tribute.
  — Include what lost person would have wanted for child in the future and tie to goals.

- Identify reminders of loss and help child develop coping skills for reminders (Layne, Saltzman, Savjak, & Pynoos, 1999).
  — Predict future times of sadness as normal and tied to anniversary dates, holidays, etc.
  — Help child give self permission to feel loss including emptiness, anger, sadness, yearning.
  — Normalize reactions as part of grief; being human by definition means to grieve over lost loved ones, not a sign of pathology or weakness.
  — Plan for how to cope when reminded of losses (triggers): who to talk to, self-soothing, imagery, use of life book to remember positive lessons.
- Help child gradually shift relationship to deceased as one to memory (Wolfelt, 1991).
- Help child identify, develop, and commit to new relationships.
- List significant people remaining or possible in child's life and how they help child.
- Help child use losses to develop new strengths and understanding from losses:
  — "If you met another boy/girl who lost someone they loved, like you did, what would you tell them?"
  — "What would you want them to know that might help them?"
  — "What would you say to them?"

Memorialize a lost person with action that builds on positive lessons inspired by that person, e.g., making the world better by raising money for cancer; speaking out against cigarette promotion to children or pressure to use drugs.

Check to see if children and caring adults have developed resources listed in Chapter 25 and also whether child's Personal Power ratings are higher than child's Knots. If not, provide additional practice on building missing skills or supplementing missing resources.

Pitfalls

- Therapist expects child to know facts about the past, rather than working together as detectives and pulling in past, current, and future caring adults to help.
- Therapist asks a child to share feelings in words when the child is too distressed about past events.

Troubleshooting

If . . .	Then . . .
Past events **trigger trauma reactions**	Triggers can be valuable clues for identifying needed safety plans and beginning work on overcoming painful memories that impair attachments. With this perspective, signs of avoidance or emotional reactions can be welcomed. Emphasize self-soothing activities and reinforcement of how the child is in a different position now, accentuating safety factors that have been put in place, e.g., a new home, a parent aware of the danger, other caring adults watching over child, alarm systems, a guard dog, etc.
Parents and guardians do not validate their own responsibility for child's losses, moves, or painful events	Parents may have difficulty validating their responsibility for child's losses and moves, e.g., a parent's drinking leading to foster care placement. Engage parents to attune to the child's feelings by harmonizing on the glockenspiel with child's note for each loss or move, or by drawing and sharing their own picture, "blues" chord, or action pose for the loss. The parent's drawing, chord, or action pose may then provide an opening to foster shared grief, recognizing how the child and the parent/guardian have experienced losses.

If . . .	Then . . .
Child is **too uncomfortable to share certain events**	Utilize "blocks" and areas of discomfort shown by child to guide later work, e.g., in Chapter 7, after child has developed greater security and trust with therapist and caring adults. Once a child learns to trust a therapist, minidramas can be enacted (after Hughes, 1998; Becker-Weidman, 2002) in which child is invited to ask the therapist, acting as a previous parent figure, the questions they have never been able to ask. e.g., "Why did a previous foster parent send me away and keep my sister?"
Child is **not aware why he or she moved**	Therapists should check with other family members, authorities, and records on what is known, then work to make it safe enough for child to learn what happened.
Parent misrepresents what happened	A parent or guardian may describe what happened in a false manner to cover shame or painful events the adult cannot face honestly. For instance, a father may say that he was repeatedly "sick" during different years of his life, when the parent was in fact living on the streets, using drugs, incarcerated, or in a series of drug programs. If an adult misrepresents the truth, therapists can ask to talk to the adult privately and point out how facing the truth is an essential part of trauma recovery. And, adults can help children grow stronger by modeling how even painful events can be faced. Often, children know when family members are distorting the truth. It is important that the child see that therapists can "say the words" (after Schlosberg, in Kagan & Schlosberg, 1989) and handle the truth. Otherwise, the child will learn that the therapist, like other family members, cannot deal with what really happened, and thus cannot be counted on to help the child and caring adults to overcome past traumas.

Checkpoints

_____ Child organizes information about his or her life in a meaningful order including happy memories and tough times.

_____ Child develops an understanding of the impact of trauma and how people in his or her family have used skills and values to recover and grow stronger.

_____ Before moving on to Chapter 8, therapists, caring adults, and children have developed resources listed in Chapter 25 and child's Personal Power ratings are higher than child's Knots and at least a "5."

Chapter 8

Through the Tough Times

Objectives

Accentuate awareness of skills, understanding, and allies (caring adults) to foster children's courage and power to manage triggers or any repetitions of difficult times in the past.

Use creative arts to help children share, progressively more difficult memories and how they could utilize skills, reasoning, and the help of caring adults to master tough times from the past including their toughest time.

Desensitize distressing reactions to tough times.

Integrate feelings, thoughts, and actions within stories of overcoming tough times.

Overview

Tough times are introduced as something everyone experiences, from movie stars, champion athletes, sports stars, cultural heroes, to therapists, family members and caring adults. The emphasis in this chapter is on learning and growing with the support of mentors, caring adults, family members, friends, and other allies. Activities are designed to counter expectations and messages that children should have been able to do better in the past to overcome hardships or help their families, or that they have failed, defining themselves forever as bad, mentally ill, or weak.

Children are encouraged to first share a time that was just a "little bit" hard. Emphasis is placed on what helped a child get through that tough time and what the child learned from that experience, now that the child is older and wiser. Chapter 8 focuses on solutions and developing "healing stories" (Figley, 1989) for difficult times, including what a child saw, heard, thought, and did, what was most difficult, emphasizing what a child would now do, as a story or movie, scene by scene, to overcome the nightmares of the past. Children are then encouraged to use the

Real Life Heroes: Practitioner's Manual
doi:10.1300/5639_14

same process with a memory of a time they learned an important lesson, another tough time, an image of all their problems combined into one picture, and their toughest time. Encourage children to utilize imagery, movies, and other creative arts activities to show how problems from the past could be managed with the broadened perspective and increased skills that they have developed along with help from caring adults.

Chapter 8 accentuates images of how children have grown and become stronger, including opportunities for them to share in pictures, words, movement, or music how they would handle troubling situations now that they are older. Therapists can use this chapter to work step by step to desensitize progressively more painful memories, incorporating self-soothing, thought stopping, reframing, and distancing techniques.

Therapists can utilize the skills and confidence developed in Chapter 8 to help each child share traumatic memories including drawing, adding tones, enacting an action pose, and finally, a story of the child and the child's allies defeating the child's toughest time. The workbook format frames this as another confidence-building exercise, which is part of a structured curriculum, and helps avoid triggering overwhelming anxiety.

Later in the chapter, children are invited to reassess their own powers and to incorporate their strengths into a game card representing them. The space for the child's self representation is larger than the space for a sketch of the child's "monster." The emphasis in these exercises is on what could overcome the child's monster.

Chapter 8 also reminds children of how heroes, in real life, feel scared and make mistakes, including hurting others, and how heroes transform themselves by developing courage, owning what they did, and by helping others. Since traumatized children are often constricted by feelings of guilt and shame, they are encouraged to share ways they've hurt others and take steps to apologize and make up for what they did. This should include a safety plan to prevent the child from repeating past harm to others.

Therapists can use Chapter 8 to reinforce how children heal within a nurturing relationship with a caring adult. For instance, a young child who scrapes her knee is comforted with a parent's supportive arm along with care for the wound, "magic" Band-Aids, and reassurance. Caring adults show children that they are not alone. Within the embrace of a caring adult, children learn how to deal with pain, step by step, beginning with validation, cleansing, treating, protecting, and guidance to prevent future injuries (Kagan, 2004b).

Often, children will begin to share parts of trauma stories in Chapter 8, if not earlier, in the workbook, e.g., after they share positive memories about a significant person in their lives. When children have a safe caring relationship with an adult and have developed sufficient self-soothing and emotional regulation skills (see checklist in Chapter 25), therapists can welcome these pieces of stories and encourage children with invitations to share their feelings and what they were thinking and doing when events occurred. Chapter 8 then provides an opportunity to process these events in a structured and recordable manner, documenting the children's progress in developing the courage to share traumas and skills and resources to reduce the power of the traumatic memories that have afflicted their lives.

Trust in a therapist, and any caring adult present, is essential for trauma processing. Therapists and caring adults connect to a child and build trust by demonstrating over time that they truly want to know what the child experienced. In child traumatic stress and complex trauma, this means knowing the often fragmented memories of witnessing and experiencing conflicting emotions, intense intimacy and pain, and good times that led to violence and terror. Children often respond well when they see, feel, and hear nonverbal and verbal messages from therapists that demonstrate, e.g., "I want to know more about what happened. . . . What were you feeling? . . . What were you saying to yourself inside your head? . . ." (Deblinger, 2005).

Since traumatized children are particularly sensitive to nuances in adults' tone of voice, posture, gestures, and facial expressions, therapists need to be able to both attune to hurt children (and adults) and at the same time keep themselves safe. Therapists must feel secure enough to truly "want to know." Part of this comes from training and understanding that facing and reintegrating painful memories is essential for trauma therapy. Therapist self-protection, as in all trauma work, is essential, including support from supervisors, administrators, and consultants. In order for a therapist to create a "sanctuary" in which trauma processing can occur, the therapist needs to work within an environment that is safe and supportive—the opposite of the neglect and abuse that drives most child traumatic stress. Implementation of principles of the Sanctuary model (Bloom, 1997) are highly recommended in mental health and child and family service organizations.

Therapists' confidence plays a major role in fostering the courage of children and caring adults to reduce the toxicity of traumas. Confidence can be enhanced with an understanding of how exposure therapies have been proven highly effective when clients experience images of past traumas long enough to reduce distress (Rothbaum & Schwartz, 2002). At the same time, short exposures that do not allow time for habituation and reduction of anxiety may increase threat avoidance and trauma reactions.

Effective exposure therapies involve repetition (Rothbaum & Schwartz, 2002) and should foster self-control by clients in setting the pace for work. Asking the child for details should be minimized in the early phases of work, which is when the child is not yet feeling safe with the therapist and distress is typically the highest. However, over the course of sessions, it is important that the therapist elicit as much detail as possible, especially about the child's toughest time, in order to promote habituation. Avoiding painful details may seem kind but it prevents emotional processing and re-integration of traumatic memories. Details include the sounds, smells, words, tone of voice, dress, and the child's reactions. Sharing the complete trauma helps put it within the child's control, rather than reinforcing its power as something that the child cannot dare to say out loud or remember. It is also important to help children relax before the end of every session, and, if possible, to end sessions with a fun activity.

In summary, Chapter 8 utilizes a series of nonverbal and verbal communications to overcome threat avoidance following traumas. Children learn that previously unbearable memories can be managed with help from caring adults and that thoughts and feelings can be modulated without returning to the overwhelming distress of traumatic events.

Step by Step

Remind children of their identified heroes from movies, literature, popular icons, neighbors and family, and stories, demonstrating how everyone faces hard times and usually fails many times before learning how to succeed. We learn through our mistakes.

Encourage children to see how much they have learned and grown in strength and size since they were little. "What are some things that you know now that can help, for yourself, or other children? Who could help them?" Consider bringing safe caring adults into sessions if this can enhance a child's confidence without constricting expression.

Suggest and practice detachment (distancing) techniques:

- The child imagines watching a scene on a movie screen from the back of a large theater or imagines watching through a thick window (five inches of bulletproof glass), while the child sits comfortably in a speeding train (Shapiro, 2001).
- Use superhero or game card images to help child feel protected from stressful memories and empowered with the help of allies to remain safe. For example, "if (the child's favorite hero) was with you now, and you saw ____, what would you do?" Boundaries around cards can be painted with dark, wide ink.

- Bring up strong images of sitting close to friends, protective family members, and other caring adults, while imagining a tough time.

For each of the tough times elicited, use creative storytelling techniques with music, video, movement, pretend radio interviews, puppet or doll enactments, or psychodrama, emphasizing development of viable solutions (Gardner, 1975).

- Act out themes from child's memories in different ways, e.g., mini-dramas.
- Explore how the child's heroes would have handled similar situations.
- Play out different endings to child's stories.

When children share parts of a trauma story, therapists (after Cohen et al., 2003), can invite them to develop a detailed story including thoughts, actions, and feelings. Children often respond well to direct invitations that let them know that the therapist wants to know the whole experience, the good parts *and* the tough times, *and* that the therapist can experience children's sharing of the experience without shaming or abandoning them. Direct messages building on the therapist-child relationship often work well to elicit a child's complete experience. Deblinger (2005), for instance, will invite children to share a complete story by sharing personal interest e.g., : "I'd like know more about that. . . What happened next? What happened right before? . . . Then what happened?" Use body-image questions to help children share their physical experience of an event, e.g., "If you scanned over your body from your toes to your belly to your head, what were you feeling? What was your heart doing? Your stomach?"

After completing the child's third tough time (see Chapter 8), ask child to sketch a three-picture story including: (1) the child with skills and powers, (2) the child's "toughest time ever," and (3) the child overcoming "toughest time."

- Begin by asking the child to draw a picture of himself or herself with all the skills and powers and everyone he or she can think of who could help the child. Remind child to practice FREEDOM (Ford & Russo, 2006) skills (see Chapter 24), e.g., "Think of who could help you. What can keep you calm? What tools and skills would you bring with you? How is your life different now?" Guide child to add details, color, and strong rhythm, intonation, and an action pose to enrich drawing.
- Next, ask child to draw a picture of his or her "toughest time ever." The child can use a simple pencil for this.
- Finally, ask the child to sketch a picture of himself or herself and all the child's allies fighting off the toughest time. The third picture will ideally show how caring adults and the child have implemented a safety plan and will accentuate the child's skills and power. Encourage the child to make this drawing the strongest, accentuating symbols of strength.
- Separate sheets should be provided for these pictures. This allows the child to feel free to start over, to add other tough times, or to crumple up pictures that are too difficult.
- After the child has drawn all three pictures, ask the child to go back and utilize sounds from the glockenspiel and an Action Pose to share how they felt and what they did in each picture.
- Afterward, ask the child to share in words what happened in each picture including a beginning, a middle, and an end for each story. Ask the child to describe feelings and thoughts. "What was worst moment, the worst part" (after Cohen et al., 2003)? "What could help (the child) feel better?" For each picture, invite the child to elaborate and expand on solutions. The child's narrative should be written down or recorded and kept with the pictures. A title sheet can be added, e.g., *My Toughest Time* and these pictures can be preserved as a separate booklet to accompany the life storybook or be kept in a special safe place.

For each tough time, ask child to continue to use rhythm, music, or action poses along with self-soothing steps, e.g., deep breathing, safe place imagery, SOS (Ford & Russo, 2006), until child feels Knots Thermometer rating at a "3" or less and Personal Power Thermometer rating higher than their Knots.

- Encourage caring adults to demonstrate understanding and acceptance of what led a child to act as he or she did in the past and to work with a child to develop resources to defeat the child's toughest times.

Pitfalls

- Children perceive therapists becoming too rushed, stressed, or anxious to help them overcome tough times.
- Ending sessions before child has an opportunity to work with tough times long enough to reduce distressful reactions.
- Children repeat the same traumatic experience over and over without learning how they can control how they remember what happened, reduce stress, and without developing images of themselves as heroes overcoming tough times rather than victims, forever doomed, damaged, or on the verge of becoming destroyed.

Troubleshooting

If . . .	Then . . .
Children **hesitate, pull back, look away,** or appear to resist sharing first tough time	A child will likely respond to the first task in Chapter 8 by thinking of a frightening incident, even though the directions ask the child to consider an incident that is only just "a little bit" difficult. The child may pull back, look away, or appear to be resisting as he or she thinks of a way to avoid dealing with a very painful memory. Remind the child to pick any kind of incident from today, yesterday, or any time, any place. The therapist's confidence is crucial in demonstrating that the child can become stronger than *tough times* and that the therapist will guide the child, step-by-step.
Children **believe they are alone or their experiences were never shared by others**	Encourage children to read books that normalize specific experiences. See "Heroes Library" (Chapter 16). Consider these references based on Cohen et al. (2003): Also, recommend these resources: • Sexual abuse, *Please Tell* (Jessie, 1991) • Parental separation due to child abuse, parental substance abuse, or hospitalization, *All Kinds of Separation* (Cunningham, 1992) • Crime, *It's My Life* (Alexander, 1993c), *All My Dreams* (Alexander, 1993a) • Homicide, *It Happened in Autumn* (Alexander, 1993b) • Traumatic death, *When I Remember* (Alexander, 1993d)

If . . .	Then . . .
Children enact or express **beliefs that they are bad, weak, damaged, or evil** because of what they did or what happened	Address expectations based on the developmental age of the child when traumas occurred. For instance, if a five-year-old experienced domestic violence including knife threats to her mother and the child then adopted beliefs she needed to always guard and protect her mother and blamed herself for failing to protect her mother, ask the child, e. g. "What can a five-year-old do when a man is holding a knife? Was the five-year-old really responsible for what a woman did? Also address children's attributions and accentuate examples of how children have grown physically, mentally, and also expanded their ties to other positive children. Reinforce how different the child and her life is now compared to the time that traumatic events took place. Bring in positive caring adults, or messages from powerful adults, e.g., clergy, extended family members, who will challenge dysfunctional beliefs and attributions.
Children's **allies are not seen as strong enough** by child to ward off fears of renewed traumas	Bring in additional supportive individuals child trusts. Encourage caring adults to demonstrate how they have grown and have made their lives different. Help caring adults to watch for nonverbal signals to child that they are not yet safe.
Children **perceive adults as not allowing memories** of how adults have failed as well as succeeded, or how adults have abused, neglected, or abandoned as well as helped others	Bridging gaps that have formed between caring adults and children requires acknowledgement and over time, acceptance of both positive and negative memories, including feelings associated with parents who both cared for and may at times have hurt children directly or indirectly. Healing from trauma requires acceptance of what happened, the good and the bad. To do this, children need a secure position and support from significant adults to share how significant adults in their lives may have been both caring and abusive at different times. Children need to experience that caring adults accept that the child may carry conflicting feelings and beliefs about a previous caretaker, e.g., both love and terror, or adoration and rage. This is especially important when children have lived with neglect and have developed chaotic, disorganized attachments.
Children present as **more anxious than expected**	Review the Resource Checklist (Chapter 25) and check for missing resources, safety plans that are not in place or sufficient, any threats regarding disclosure, or changes that have decreased a child's capacity to cope with stressors.
Children **balk at sharing toughest time ever**	Cohen et al. (2003) provide detailed guidelines for helping children tell the story of specific traumas. This begins with explaining to children and their guardians how writing a book about the trauma is like cleaning out a cut. It hurts at first but each time you work on it, the pain goes down. And, cleaning out the cut reduces pain of what happened. The therapist will help the child to make sure that the child only feels a little pain at any time. And, like all stories, the story of what happens has a beginning, a middle, and an end. The child can choose what page of his or her story to talk about first.

If . . .	Then . . .
	In this model, children are asked to describe what they remember happening without interruption. The therapist may write or type the child's story.
	Afterward, the therapist can ask questions to add details to the story including questions about what the child was thinking and feeling at different points in the story. In the *Real Life Heroes* format, this can be enhanced by asking children to sketch pictures, express feelings, tap rhythms, and make up chords, action poses, and enactments to nonverbally express how they feel.
	Having children read aloud what they have written helps desensitize and can be used to promote validation and support. After several repetitions, the child's emotional distress should go down. Use of relaxation techniques is important in this process.
	After the child has added thoughts and feelings to the story, ask the child to share the 'worst moment" (see Cohen et al., 2003).
	The child is reinforced at the end of each session, e.g., with food, praise, and a positive activity.
Children **remain anxious** after work on Chapter 8	Utilize additional therapies that incorporate nonverbal trauma processing, e.g., EMDR adapted for children (Greenwald, 1999; Shapiro, 2001).
Children share experiences with therapist but appear **too anxious to share experiences with caring adults**	If child wants to express experiences to an adult but is too frightened to do this directly, consider nondirect means of sharing. For example, invite child to make a phone call to therapist's answering machine or tape recorder in which child is invited to talk into telephone and answer questions from therapist about more sensitive issues (Purdy, 2003). Child can then listen to the tape and it can be transcribed and shared with people the child trusts.
Parents or caring **adults block expression** of tough times	Adults may be coping in their own lives with denial and avoidance and see this as essential for getting by. Or, adults may believe that sharing personal pain in any way leads to weakness or moral failure. Optimally, caring adults can be reminded of the psychoeducation materials presented earlier, stressing how trauma impacts children (and adults). It is often helpful to utilize descriptions and research from studies of soldiers and survivors of natural disasters as well as family violence. References for adults on the impact of trauma may be helpful; see, for example, *Wounded Angels: Lessons from Children in Crisis* (Kagan, 2003). In many cases, it is important to help adults reassess their own fears and goals and to recontract to help children become heroes rather than remain stuck reliving traumas.
Children, or parents, insist that **no one talk about "family business"**	Leaving a story untold can be compared to leaving a cut uncleaned and untreated (Cohen et al., 2003). The result is often a chronic infection. Healing cannot occur in this context and the child and parent's goals for the child cannot be achieved.
	For many families, an emphasis on building on the strengths and caring, when present, can help engage reluctant parents. In other families, neglect may be dominant and court orders will be needed for real change, protection, and healthy development of children.

If . . .	Then . . .
Additional safety plans, skills, or supportive resources are needed	One of the advantages of following a structured protocol is that assigned activities will bring out unresolved issues that continue to trouble a child but were not known by caring adults or service providers. Therapists can welcome a child's hesitation, or resistance, and use the child's behaviors as clues to what can help increase the child's security and strength *(Personal Power)* to a level that would allow the child to move forward. This may mean developing greater self-soothing skills, but more likely, dysfunctional beliefs or lingering threats will need to be addressed.

Often, a child may be able to move forward when safe, caring adults are engaged to join sessions. With an arm behind the child, and reassurance, children may be able to move forward. Starting with rhythm, tonality, and drawing often helps. In other cases, role-plays dramatizing how caring adults will protect a child from past perpetrators (see Hughes, 1997) is very helpful. |

Checkpoints

_____ Child utilizes skills and ties to caring adults (allies) to manage reminders or repetitions of difficult times in the past.

_____ Child shares most difficult memories without becoming overwhelmed and is able to express what is different now that would prevent retraumatization.

_____ Child expresses remorse and begins to implement a plan for apologizing and making appropriate restitution for one thing she regrets.

Chapter 9

Into the Future

Objectives

Promote development of child's positive beliefs about self, extending into the future.

Encourage child's expression of involvement in enduring positive and nurturing relationships.

Incorporate image of child helping others into child's identity.

Overview

In heroic stories (Campbell, 1968), the transformed hero returns with newfound knowledge or wealth, the "boon," that can benefit the community in the future. Chapter 9 provides an opportunity for children to incorporate skills and positive beliefs about themselves into images of their hopes for the future. Children are encouraged in this process to continue to help others, which is a key factor in building self-esteem and in developing into the citizens every community needs.

The Greek definition of hero, "to serve and protect," (Vogler, 1998) can be reinforced and utilized to strengthen ties between the child and people the child cares about. Similarly, elements of the child's favorite heroic stories involving helping others can be stressed, e.g., "With great power, comes great responsibility" from *The Amazing Spiderman* (Lee, 1963). In this way, therapists and caring adults help the child to grow into a caring adult.

Step by Step

Encourage child to visualize his or her life as a whole. Review time line from Chapter 7, the ups and the downs, and have child draw or enact future goals for self.

Ask child to draw or enact self utilizing desired skills and attributes in the future.

- Accentuate how child sees self helping others.
- Have child share important lessons learned in the course of completing workbook.
- Help child incorporate the skills and sensitivities developed to survive and overcome trauma as special attributes that they can use to help others in the future.

Pitfalls

- Children perceive messages from family members or service providers that, despite all their work, they remain victims forever, or they are entitled to special treatment forever more because of how they were so "damaged."
- Future stories focus on child alone without positive, enduring relationships.

Real Life Heroes: Practitioner's Manual
Published by The Haworth Press, Inc., 2007. All rights reserved.
doi:10.1300/5639_15

Troubleshooting

If . . .	Then . . .
Child has **trouble visualizing a future**	Encourage child to visualize life as a book or movie, moving from year to year, and highlighting key goals and relationships (see Greenwald, 1999). Remind child how many successful books or movies (e.g., *Harry Potter* or *Spiderman*) have sequels, many become better than the first books or movies in the series.
Child appears to be **superficial,** or to show little feeling about workbook activities	Elicit a greater range of perspective and feeling with different art materials, e.g., paints, clay, musical expression with a different instrument, e.g., a bongo drum; or movement activities, e.g., enactments of scenes child creates, or sculptures. Invite child to compare own stories to books, movies, stories child enjoys.
Caretakers **treat child as fragile** or requiring special treatment with "kid gloves"	Children need to see that parents and other caring adults believe they are "normal" and can be strong. Children watch for these beliefs in the way they are treated by caring adults.

Checkpoints

_____ Child develops positive images and beliefs about self extending into the future.
_____ Child incorporates helping others into identity.
_____ Child expresses confidence in attaining goals.

Chapter 10

Completing the Book:
Telling the Story

Objectives

Help child to express an organized an integrated story of his or her life.
Help child to share his or her story with caring adults.

Overview

After completion of the life storybook, encourage children to write an integrated life story. This can be presented as part of the heroes quest, in terms of sharing what the child has learned and gained in a way that helps the child, family members, and other people in the child's community.

The child's narrative life story provides a measure of whether the child has been able to integrate painful events into his or her life. After completing the life storybook and rebuilding the positive parts of their lives, most children are able to see that traumatic events, even repeated traumas, were limited to certain times, places, and interactions, a small part of their entire experience. The objective is not for children to forget what happened, but rather to be able to share a coherent, integrated account of their lives in which traumatic events are no longer all consuming. From a concrete perspective, the child's Personal Power will become much stronger than the Knots associated with a specific or even repeated traumas.

Completion of the book can be celebrated with a ceremony honoring the child as "author" including autographed copies for the family to save in a special location. A parent can offer to lock the book away in a secure place, to be read again whenever the child wishes. Certificates can be framed and combined with photographs of the child and caring adults who helped the child.

Children may also be honored by asking them to share their life stories with younger children or children who have recently experienced similar "tough times" (after White & Epston, 1990; Freedman & Combs, 1996). With consent from children and guardians, this could include donating a copy to a special library after names and other identifying details have been changed.

Real Life Heroes: Practitioner's Manual
Published by The Haworth Press, Inc., 2007. All rights reserved.
doi:10.1300/5639_16

Step by Step

If the child did not share a story of a major traumatic event in Chapter 8, encourage the child to share a "trauma narrative" (after Cohen et al., 2003) provided he or she has developed the safety and resources necessary to share painful memories (see Chapter 25). Completion of the life storybook usually provides the skills and resources children need to be able to share what they experienced in detail, something they may not have been able to do before. Very often, children do this spontaneously, as they work on life storybook chapters.

Often, when children have experienced multiple traumas, they will begin by sharing incidents that were less stressful, watching carefully to see if therapists and caring adults can handle dealing with their experiences without becoming harsh, shaming, or abandoning, or otherwise, triggering deep-seated fears. Children often need to hear, several times, that therapists truly want to know about everything they experienced, even the worst experiences. Invitations from the therapist to talk about these experiences, often work to elicit stories the child has been holding back. Deblinger (2005) suggests giving children a message that connects to this implicit understanding between therapist and child. For instance, in the case of a child who experienced repeated incidents of physical or sexual violence during night times, the therapist could say, "You know, I also thought it would be helpful to talk about one night that was especially scary, or one time that was different, that stood out some way, that was different."

Ask children to compose a narrative, audiotape, or videotape of their entire life from birth to their current age as a summary and wrapup to the *Real Life Heroes* workbook. A word processing program helps or the blank pages at the end of the workbook can also be used. The narrative can be of any length and can be presented in many ways, e.g., a written movie or as a videotaped interview with the child.

- Utilize the life events chart or road map from Chapter 7 as an outline to guide the story.
- Encourage children to highlight both good and bad times emphasizing: what was learned, strengths that helped them overcome problems, how they helped others, the children's goals for the future, what they want to learn, and how they will help others.
- Encourage children to integrate thoughts, actions, and feelings.

Invite children to create their own title pages, like books in the library. Heavy paper is recommended. Title pages can then be laminated. Children can also include a "Dedication" as a way of thanking special people in their lives. For an attractive book cover (Scheele, 2005), bind the pages together between two pieces of process board using book thread and a child-safe stitching needle with no sharp point. Prepare the covers in advance by having an adult punch three holes into the pages using a pushpin or a hole punch. After board and pages are stitched together, a child-safe glue can be added to help secure the outside binding. Cloth book tape can then be added to the whole length of binding while the glue is still wet. Finally, encourage children to add a photograph of themselves to the back with a brief paragraph under the heading, "About the Author."

Invite children to share their storybook with safe, validating adults and children in their families and, as appropriate, with other service providers, mentors, and clergy. Introduce storybooks as including both good times and tough times, and how books highlight the importance of caring, safety, courage, and commitment with respect and thanks for caring adults who helped child along the way.

Invite children to share their stories, or allow portions to be shared anonymously, to help younger children going through similar experiences.

Maintain a back-up copy of the life storybook in a safe place. The original can be laminated and bound. Keeping two or three copies is highly recommended in order to preserve a child's memories and provide a resource for the child in later years.

Review safety and coping steps to deal with predictable problems and reminders of traumas.

Pitfalls

- Narrative or summary life stories focus on negative traumas rather than accentuating how child and caring adults overcame past traumas and reinforcing the strengths of the child, caring adults, families, and ethnic heritage.
- Child's life storybook is left accessible, or shared, with adults or family members who do not meet safety criteria or without permission of child and a safe guardian.

Troubleshooting

If . . .	Then . . .
Child continues to **balk at sharing a narrative of toughest time** in any modality	Recheck for safety concerns: child may need court orders not yet in place, resolution of family or criminal court proceedings, return to a now safe home, or placement into a potential adoptive home before trauma processing can occur. See Cohen et al. (2003) and Kolko & Swenson (2002) for other practice recommendations.
Child **fears** that completion of the workbook will mean **an end to work with the therapist** or other caring adults	When therapeutic relationships must end, it is important to respect the loss this entails and a child's fears of losing important people. Completing the book should be viewed as another point in a child's journey in life, rather than an end point. It's important to accentuate who will be continuing to help children as they mature, i.e., committed caring adults.
Child **believes therapist wants to be done with child,** leaving child behind	The therapist's role as a guide and mentor can be highlighted along with how the therapist will keep the memory of the child's accomplishments alive through pictures or a copy of the storybook. Therapists can point out what they have learned from work with child and, if appropriate, invite child to send letters about special events in child's life to therapist's agency or professional office.
Child was successful in a time-limited program or at an agency, but **lacks positive roles in own community**	It is very important to ensure that each child develops positive roles in his or her community through involvement in areas of interest and talent and with the support of family members, mentors, coaches, etc. Wherever possible, reintegration of children into their neighborhood, school, and community should be included as part of therapeutic work along with follow-up after discharge to work on any problems that develop.
Guardian or funding source requests termination of therapy before completion of workbook because child has stabilized	Often, county social services or other authorities, grappling with budget deficits, will pressure family preservation and mental health services to terminate as soon as overt dangerous behavior subsides. It is important to advocate for the time and sessions necessary for trauma processing and reintegration Stopping trauma therapy at the point of behavioral "stabilization" leaves children and families at high risk of renewed cyclical symptoms as well as the prospect of much more costly placement or replacement.

If . . .	Then . . .
Parent or guardian becomes too busy for children to finish workbook after taking on a new job	For important and valid reasons, parents and guardians may make changes in their own lives that interfere with therapy, e.g., taking on a new job with greater hours for higher pay or career advancement. SDeek the parent's or guardian's permission to continue work with the child with sessions at school, or seeing a child at a babysitter's home. This way, children and families can complete the process. Parents and guardians may still be able to participate in limited sharing sessions, and thus help children complete work on reintegration.

Checkpoints

After completing the life storybook, children demonstrate ability to:

_____ Identify people who have cared about them at different ages
_____ Identify people who could help them with problems now or the future
_____ Express memories of nurture and strength, as well as memories of *tough times* including feelings, perceptions, and beliefs
_____ Share stories of how they and significant family members overcame *tough times* including correction of beliefs that fostered shaming and self-denigration
_____ Describe, with age-appropriate words, how what they did was related to what they experienced, a "healing story" (after Figley, 1989) including a meaningful life story
_____ Accept physiological reactions to trauma reminders
_____ Identify and practice plans for how to protect self and loved ones if traumatic situations begin again
_____ Understand own skills and strengths including behaviors learned in *tough times* and goals for strengthening skills
_____ Describe how they have helped other people and how they would like to help other people in the future

By working with children on their life storybook, caring adults demonstrate ability to:

_____ Identify people who, in the past or present, will continue to protect, guide, and nurture child
_____ Identify people who, in the past, will continue to validate a child's experiences
_____ Identify critical losses for a child and help child to grieve
_____ Identify a child's fears and develop and implement safety plans
_____ Help a child replace destructive beliefs with positive assertions
_____ Understand how a child's behaviors were developed within past relationships and experiences and can be changed
_____ Provide opportunities for children to develop skills in communication, relationships with siblings, parents, peers, teachers, and authorities, as well as special talents

PART III:
HANDOUTS AND ADAPTATIONS—
TOOLS FOR THE JOURNEY

Chapter 11

Adaptation for Adolescents

The *Real Life Heroes Storybook* was written especially for children between the ages of six and twelve. In pilot studies, the workbook has been found to work well with adolescents who are developmentally in this age range, especially thirteen- to fourteen-year-olds. The workbook has also been effective with older adolescents with adaptations of the themes addressed on each page, use of group activities, and more age-appropriate creative arts. Removing or replacing the child-centered graphics in the workbook has often been sufficient to engage older adolescents who are struggling developmentally with challenges addressed in this curriculum. Pages can also be pulled out for group activities or individual therapy sessions.

The challenge *and* the appeal of using the workbook with adolescents with traumatic stress centers on adolescents' drive to free themselves from their families and establish their own identities at the same time that they are often struggling with childhood traumas and unmet dependency needs. The workbook addresses this dual challenge, especially with adolescents who function developmentally at a younger age and adolescents who were traumatized as children and whose social and emotional development was stymied.

With adolescents in foster care and independent living programs, just as with younger children, it is essential to bring in positive supportive adults and peers. It is helpful as part of assessments, to utilize some of the questions from the Important People Questionnaire (Chapter 18) and invite older adolescents to bring to contracting and review conferences caring adults they trust, or if necessary, to include these people on a regular basis by telephone or videoconferencing.

In review conferences, it is helpful to focus on: adolescents' primary goals; progress toward goals; anything getting in the way; and what can be done to help them overcome obstacles and achieve goals. With this strength- and goal-centered framework, adolescents are often willing to encourage caring adults to participate in activities, and, in turn, caring adults can be engaged to help monitor, coach, and guide adolescents including serving as resources to help identify, prevent, and, if necessary, cope with triggers to chronic trauma behavior cycles. Caring adults can also provide encouragement for adolescents to utilize their understanding and strengths to accomplish their goals and move away from repetitive behavior cycles that reactivate traumatic reactions.

To engage adolescents, appeal to their greater understanding and abstract reasoning ability as teenagers and, at the same time, to their ability to work on materials at multiple levels with creative arts. Therapists have found it helpful to:

- Encourage youths to take the life storybook and recreate it in their own way, e.g., making a movie, writing a series of rap songs, or writing a journal, poetry, or an autobiography, e.g., "My World, My Way." The chapters and tasks can serve as an outline to break up the work into manageable sections, just as the author of a book or the director of a movie divides up a

Real Life Heroes: Practitioner's Manual
Published by The Haworth Press, Inc., 2007. All rights reserved.
doi:10.1300/5639_17

project into segments. The nine chapters of the *Life Storybook* can present an initial outline for an autobiography.

- Invite youths to go "back in time" and imagine themselves at a younger age; respond to workbook exercises, and then work on the book at their current age. For instance, they could imagine themselves at age six *and* fifteen, completing pages the way they used to feel and think when things were very hard. Then, invite youths to contemplate how they feel and understand situations from the vantage point of their current age.
- Ask youths to complete the book as a gift for younger siblings or as a way of helping younger children who have experienced situations resembling what happened in their lives. At the same time, use the workbook to develop special competence in an area of strength or interest, e.g., singing, art, sports. This may take on even more significance for adolescents and can lead to mentoring relationships and opportunities for adolescents to help others, while at the same time, boosting their own self esteem.
- Invite youths to, just for fun, try out something written for younger children; children who went through what they did when they were younger, *even though* they are *much* older now.
- Substitute "dreams," skills, and real-life problems for the more child-centered magic tricks, dragons, and monsters in the workbook (Peacock & Hawkins, 2004).
- Break up sections or pages of the workbook into separate handouts for sessions or group activities, rather than using the workbook as a whole.
- Present materials to youths in a white folder (Peacock & Hawkins, 2004) and provide materials to decorate it encouraging self-expression and identity. Youths could be asked to decorate the front when they start and the back when they finish, creating a beginning and ending ritual.
- Utilize group arts and crafts projects to identify significant people in their lives and resources they can call upon for help to achieve their goals and manage stressful situations. For example, in groups (Rappaport, 2006), use photographs or drawings of favorite people to create three-dimensional frame cubes and make shields with collages with drawings of symbols of strength and important people who can help youths.

As part of growing up and establishing their own identities, adolescents become very sensitive to peers and their behavior is shaped a great deal by their involvement with positive or negative peers and informal or formal groups. Adolescents often learn with peers how to utilize abstract reasoning skills to find new ways to master old problems. Therapists can utilize adolescents' affinity for peers to shape understanding and coping skills.

Group exercises on learning to understand and overcome trauma, manage feelings (affect regulation) and develop assertive communication and problem solving skills can be very effective (see Cloitre, Koenen, Cohen, & Han, 2002; DeRosa et al., 2005; Ford & Russo, 2006; Ford et al., 2001, 2003; Ford & St. Juste, 2006; Miller, Rathus, & Linehan, 2006; Saltzman, Layne, & Pynoos, 2003.) Therapists can also use pages from the *Real Life Heroes Storybook* as a guide for group activities in which adolescents choose their own modality or work together with painting, sculpture, choreography or theatre arts.

Use of contemporary music in adolescent groups is a great way to engage youths, normalize traumatic experiences, promote expression, and create opportunities for youths to help one another using mediums they enjoy. Many popular songs address themes of overcoming traumas. Peacock & Hawkins (2004). Peacock & Hawkins (2004) used songs including "The Message" (Grandmaster Flash and Furious Five, 1982, The Sugar Hill Gang); "Slow Down" (India Arie, 2002, Voyage to India, Motown Records); "Anxiety" (Black Eyed Peas, 2003, Elephunk, Interscope Records); "Get it together" (India Arie, 2002, Voyage to India, Motown Records); and "The Miseducation of Lauryn Hill" (Lauryn Hill, 1998, The Miseducation of Lauryn Hill, Columbia). For additional suggested music, please see "Heroes Library" (Chapter 16). Adolescents can be invited to bring in some of their favorites, screening out, as necessary, any music that promotes violence, ethnic debasement, or self-abuse. Similarly, caring adults can be invited to share music that inspires them. See for instance, "In My Daugther's Eyes" (Martina McBride, 2003, Martina, BMG).

Adolescents can also be engaged to help one another develop solutions to difficult situations in their lives, e.g., being insulted by a storekeeper, being accused by a peer of trying to take away their boyfriend or girlfriend, pressure to engage in unsafe behavior, being questioned by a passing police officer. This can be done with enactments, dance, music and arts, even creation of short movies or plays. It's very important in these activities to help youths move beyond misinterpretations of other people's behaviors that lead to trauma reactions, especially perceptions that other people are targeting the youths with little or no recognition of other possibilities. For instance, the belligerence experienced from a police officer questioning youths late at night may stem from the officers' receiving urgent calls for help regarding other youths who had been violent in the same neighborhood or the officers' own personal experiences, rather than anything having to do with a particular youth.

Discussions that promote understanding of sexual, economic, or ethnic victimization can also be used to engage older youths and to help them redirect their anger into active steps that foster competence and strength and help youths break out of self-shaming. Active involvement in advocacy groups such as NOW, the NAACP, "take back the night" marches, etc., with caring adults and peers is also recommended.

The hero framework can be addressed with a focus on individuation and adolescents' drive to develop self-respect (Peacock & Hawkins, 2004); e.g., "What will it take for you to become a hero?" Emphasize personal goals and choices including identification of:

- What has helped you make good choices in the past?
- What has gotten in the way of making good choices?
- Who can you count on to tell you when you are wrong and help to make things better?
- Who helps you make good choices and do the work necessary to succeed?
- What would it take for you to become a person you respect?

For individual or group sessions, youths can be asked to make a list or draw people they respect, e.g., "Who I respect and why." Adolescents could then be asked to discuss: "In what ways are they similar to the people they respect? And, what would it take to become the 'best possible you'(Peacock & Hawkins, 2004)?"

Conversely, youths can be asked to respond to questions about people who give mixed messages, pressure others to get into trouble, or show disrespect to themselves or other people. Discussion questions could include (Peacock & Hawkins, 2004):

- What examples do you see in the news or in movies, stories, etc., about people who *say* they care but do something very different?
- Are there people in your life who said they cared but then treated you or others disrespectfully or hurt them?
- How can people manage overt disrespect?
- What can help with covert disrespect?

Fantasy activities and discussions related to the future are especially helpful with adolescents who have experienced chronic trauma and who have given up hope for change. It's helpful to expand upon Chapter 9 activities with imagery exercises about what they hope to be doing at different ages. Solution-based therapy exercises can be very useful. Youths can be asked to imagine themselves at an older age: what helped them succeed? What have they learned? What would they advise to themselves at a younger age (after Dolan, 1991)? What would be their greatest dream for the future? What would it look like? Who would be with them? What would be the smallest step toward making their dream come true? What would be a second step? These exercises can lead to step-by-step plans for making adolescents' goals come true.

- Completing the book should be viewed as another point in a youth's journey in life, rather than an end point. It's important to accentuate who will be continuing to help an adolescent as he or she matures, i.e., committed caring adults.
- The therapist's role as a guide and mentor can be highlighted along with how the therapist will keep the memory of the youth's accomplishments alive through pictures or a copy of the storybook.
- It is very important to ensure that each youth have positive roles in his or her community through involvement in areas of interest and talent and with the active support of family members, mentors, coaches, etc.
- Adolescents develop independent living skills best when they work on these skills with caring adults, e.g., cooking, paying bills, getting cars repaired, etc. Classes cannot substitute for the guidance of a caring adult (Cook, 2005).

Just as with younger children, an attachment-centered focus is essential in effective work with adolescents. Relationships change over the years and caring adults need to find ways to keep bonds and close ties with young people as they mature. Close family ties may be lost after traumatic events, especially when family members become disabled or die. It's easy then for adolescents to become detached, withdrawn, or pressed by remaining family members to grow up and move on with their lives. Governmental organizations may regard adolescents as less vulnerable or simply not eligible for protective services. In reality, this is a time of great risk, which is demonstrated by the high rate of victimization of adolescents compared to other age groups. This is also a time of great opportunity to help adolescents overcome traumas and shape positive identities as successful young adults, future parents, and citizens contributing to their communities. Life story work can play an important role in this transformation.

Chapter 12

Adaptation for Preschool Children and Children with Disabilities

The workbook can be adapted for children with moderate developmental delays or learning disabilities. For some children, narrative responses may be only a single word, while more verbal children may want to generate multipage stories for every topic. Additional guidance and help is needed for children with cognitive abilities under age six. Therapists or caring adults may need to read text to children and help them spell words, working carefully to reflect the children's responses without bias. Adults can also write out the child's dictated story on notepaper or on a word processor. Then, either the adult or the child can copy the story onto the appropriate page of *Real Life Heroes*.

Often, children with limited writing skills do better by dictating answers into a tape recorder that can later by typed and inserted into the life book. Therapists can take on the role of a radio or TV interviewer, and then use the questions on each worksheet as a mock interview that can be taped for later transcription, and, if desired, shared with caring adults.

Other children may prefer to use word processing programs to facilitate writing and editing narratives that can be pasted into the book or printed directly on the bottom of pages under pictures. Audio or videotapes can also be made to accompany the pictures, page by page.

Younger children often can be engaged to utilize puppets for storytelling and therapists or caring adults can transcribe the story enacted. Simple puppets can be constructed by having children sketch images of family members or other figures, cut them out with a child-safe scissors, and tape the images to a piece of folded cardboard. The result can be a group of puppet figures that the child owns and with which the child can act out stories from his or her own experience. As children develop broader perspectives about family members and other important people in their lives, they can change their drawings. Desensitization exercises and activities designed to boost self-esteem helps children reduce the power and intensity of frightening images while increasing the size, power, and strength of pictures of themselves, caring family members, and other positive people in their lives.

Real Life Heroes: Practitioner's Manual
Published by The Haworth Press, Inc., 2007. All rights reserved.
doi:10.1300/5639_18

Chapter 13

Adaptation for Families
with Adopted Children

Real Life Heroes works very well with older children who have been placed into preadoptive homes or with children who have been adopted after experiencing multiple moves in their lives. The workbook allows children to share their past with their new parents *and* relatives, to get help in answering questions, and to find out if their new family will accept their past experiences, affection, loyalty, grief, and wishes.

Children adopted as infants can also grow up with questions, doubts, and at times, deep-seated insecurity, if their past is shrouded in secrecy. Life story work helps children and parents to transform nonverbalized feelings of tension, fear, or sadness into pictures and words, providing a means for adoptive parents to connect with children and help them grieve. By working with children on the life storybook, adoptive parents can validate typical concerns of children and demonstrate courage and commitment to their children. Adoptive parents can show that they respect a child's natural curiosity and feelings of loyalty by helping the child learn as much as possible about his or her birth parents, or first family (or families).

If adoptive parents tell a child that they "chose" to adopt the child, the child will naturally want to know why his or her previous biological or foster parents chose *not* to keep them. Adoptive parents may be tempted to "block out" information on lost parents out of anger or fear of losing a child, or as a way of protecting a child from dealing with birth parents' medical problems, criminal actions, addictions, neglect, or rejection of a child. Other adoptive parents may feel a need to make up some excuse or justification for what previous parents have done. Neither is helpful for a child (van Gulden & Bartels-Rabb, 1995).

Adoptive parents should be encouraged to provide a balanced view with respect for children, parents, and family members. Dichotomies, such as the "good" versus the "bad" parent may be initially comforting, but often lead later on to idealization and expectations of perfection in parents and the children themselves. Children who learn to think in "black or white" terms often flip back and forth and may begin responding to their new parents as "good or bad," but never "real."

Life story work is about honesty and courage. Deep inside, children have experienced what really happened. Distortions confuse children and teach them that their parents are afraid to address and overcome what really happened.

Entering an adoptive family can mark the beginning of a new world, a special world, which incorporates new possibilities for a traumatized child including the resources to face the truth. In this special world, the greatest fears of parents and children are often tested through a series of ordeals. These determine whether this family will prove to be a variation of past losses or abandonments, or whether this new reformed family will foster a parent-child bond that includes the whole child's experience.

Real Life Heroes: Practitioner's Manual
Published by The Haworth Press, Inc., 2007. All rights reserved.
doi:10.1300/5639_19

Adopted children go through the same developmental phases and behaviors as children growing up with their birth parents. It's important for adoptive parents to understand developmental norms and to not overreact to common behaviors, e.g., a two-year-old's temper tantrums or a four-year-old's night terrors. When children who have experienced traumatic stress act out excessively, the strength of children's defiance or troubling behavior often matches the level of the traumas experienced. It's as if the child is warning would-be parents: "Do you dare to enter my world?" The child's behaviors push parents away, but at the same time, challenge parents to face the child's deepest secrets.

It helps for adoptive parents to remember that children who have felt abandoned or rejected often desperately need to remain in control. Defiance and testing is part of the child's struggle with the conflicting wish to trust again and, at the same time, deep-seated, trauma-based reactions push the child to fear and avoid any sense of dependence.

This cycle of interaction is most evident when a child tells adoptive parents, "You're not my real parents," or when children threaten to leave. "I hate you. I want to go to my 'real' parents." By overtly challenging adoptions, or adoption plans, wounded children test their beliefs, often from multiple past rejections, that "deep down, these new parents *want* me to leave." The adoptive, or preadoptive, parents' responses to the child's challenges can prove the parents' commitment over time or conversely confirm the child's deepest fears.

Accepting the challenge of adopting a traumatized child means opening oneself to the child's pain and bringing a child's struggles into one's own home. This takes tremendous courage. "To serve and protect" represents the ancient Greek definition of heroes (Vogler, 1998). Parents who adopt wounded children are truly heroes who "serve and protect," transforming the lives of hurt children and their communities.

Chapter 14

Real Life Heroes Summary

Real Life Heroes utilizes an activity-based workbook to help children with traumatic stress to build the skills and interpersonal resources needed to reintegrate painful memories and to foster healing after abuse, neglect, family violence, severe illness, losses, deaths, or abandonment. The workbook utilizes creative arts and life story work to engage children and caring adults in trauma and attachment-centered therapy and to rebuild (or build) positive, enduring relationships between hurt (and often hurting) children and adults committed to guiding children into adulthood. The curriculum integrates nonverbal and verbal modalities and helps children and caring adults move step by step from trauma narratives to life stories highlighting mastery, helping others, and nurturing relationships

Real Life Heroes was especially designed for children in child and family service programs who frequently lack safe, nurturing homes and secure relationships with caring and committed adults. The model assists therapists and family members to recover and enhance family and cultural strengths and to promote skill building, attachments, and trauma processing. The model can be used by programs and agencies as a prescriptive methodology to address primary goals including preventing placements, reuniting families, or finding alternate permanent homes for children who cannot return to biological parents.

Real Life Heroes helps children:

- Recognize heroes within their families, communities, and ethnic heritage and to develop a sense of hope that they can move past traumas
- Develop skills to identify and express feelings and manage emotions utilizing drawings, rhythm, melodies, and movement
- Use pictures, photos, and stories in a structured workbook format to tell the unique story of a child's life strengthening positive memories of caring
- Develop children's capacity and confidence to cope with past, present, and future stressors and enable troubled children to transform from victims into "heroes" within their families and communities

Interventions:

- Engage caring adults to validate children by building on the caring of family members, strengthening each child's cultural and family heritage, fostering an understanding of trauma, and reduction of shaming/blaming includeing specific steps to make it safe for children to work on healing including guidelines for involving caring adults and helping caring adults become mentors, protectors, and heroes for children
- Engage children to work chapter by chapter on building competence and a stronger identity
- Utilize activities to build critical skills to manage intense affective reactions including affect recognition and regulation, acceptance and understanding of trauma reactions, self-

Real Life Heroes: Practitioner's Manual
Published by The Haworth Press, Inc., 2007. All rights reserved.
doi:10.1300/5639_20

monitoring, working with peers and adults to overcome adversity, and helping others as a means of building self-esteem
- Utilize creative arts (drawing, color, rhythm, music, movement) to foster attunement between children and caring adults, strengthen positive memories of caring, increase capacity for problem resolution, share "tough times," and develop coping strategies strong enough to counter reminders, "triggers," to trauma reactions
- Utilize components of cognitive behavioral therapy (CBT) including psycho-education on trauma, affect regulation, social skill-training, changing dysfunctional beliefs, progressive desensitization, and telling the story by providing a structured curriculum and child-friendly workbook
- Can be easily integrated with trauma-focused therapies and home-based family preservation, therapeutic foster family, residential treatment, and juvenile justice programs

The manual and workbook were designed to prevent or treat traumatic stress with children and adolescents who function developmentally between ages six to twelve and who have experienced losses, neglect, abuse, violence, illness, or disasters including:

- children identified as abused, neglected, or PINS/JD;
- children with complex PTSD, "developmental trauma disorder";
- children at risk of placement;
- children placed into foster families, residential treatment centers, psychiatric hospitals, crisis residences, or runaway/homeless youth programs;
- families working in pre- and postadoption counseling; and
- older adolescents, preschool children, and children who have learning disabilities utilizing adaptations outlined in the manual.

The manual was designed to help therapists strengthen caring adults, or when necessary, to search for caring adults and engage them to rebuild attachments and provide long term guidance, nurture, and safe homes.

The manual also provides a curriculum that can be used as the framework for an eight- to twelve-month trauma therapy practicum for graduate students. This would ideally include an introduction to trauma for group or foster care staff, e.g., *START* (Benamati, 2004), a two-day workshop on *Real Life Heroes,* review of the *Real Life Heroes Therapist's Manual* (Kagan, 2007) and *Rebuilding Attachments for Traumatized Children* (Kagan, 2004), completion of the life storybook by the intern, and weekly supervision in use of the model by a clinical supervisor with advanced training in trauma therapy and use of this model.

Real Life Heroes meets the minimum requirements of the National Registry of Evidence-based Programs and Practices (Substance Abuse and Mental Health Services Administration) and is listed as one of the Empirically Supported Treatments and Promising Practices implemented by the National Child Traumatic Stress Network (www.nctsnet.org).

Chapter 15

Resources for Caring Adults

Parenting, Education, and Healthy Development

Brazelton, T. (1974). *Touchpoints: Your Child's Emotional and Behavioral Development, Birth to 3—The Essential Reference for the Early Years*. Cambridge, MA: Da Capo Life Long Press.

Brazelton, T. & Cramer, B. G. (1990). The Earliest Relationship. New York: Addison-Wesley.

Jensen, E. (2000). *Brain-based Learning*. San Diego: The Brain Store.

Lansky, V. (1991). *101 Ways to Make Your Child Feel Special*. Chicago: Contemporary Books.

Lansky, V. (1992). *Practical Parenting Tips*. New York: Meadowbrook Press.

Lansky, V. (1993). *Games Babies Play*. Deephaven, MN: The Book Peddlers.

Manolson, A. (1995). *You Can Make the Difference*. Toronto: Hanen Centre.

Morin, V. (1993). *Messy Activities and More*. Chicago: Chicago Review Press.

Siegel, D. & Hartzell, M. (2003). *Parenting from the Inside Out: How a Deeper Self-Understanding Can Help You Raise Children Who Thrive*. New York: JP Tarcher/Putnam.

Small, M. (1998). *Our Babies, Ourselves; How Biology and Culture Shape the Way We Parent*. New York: Anchor Books.

ZERO TO THREE (1997). *How I Grow in Your Care from Zero to Three*. Arlington, VA: National Center for Infants, Toddlers, and Families.

Attachment Research and Interventions

Ainsworth, M.D.S., Blehar, M. C., Waters, B., & Wall, S. (1978) *Patterns of Attachment: A Psychological Study of the Strange Situation*. Hillsdale, NJ: Lawrence Erlbaum.

Beringen, Z. (1994). Attachment theory and research: Application to clinical practice. *American Journal of Orthopsychiatry, 6* (3), 404-420.

Bowlby, J. (1988). *A Secure Base: Parent-Child Attachment and Healthy Human Development*. New York: Basic.

Delaney, R. (1997). *Healing Power*. Oklahoma City, OK: Woods 'N' Barnes.

Delaney, R. (1998). *Fostering Changes*. Oklahoma City, OK: Woods 'N' Barnes.

Delaney, R. (1998). *Raising Cain*. Oklahoma City, OK: Woods 'N' Barnes.

Hughes, D. (1997). *Facilitating Developmental Attachment*. Northvale, NJ: Jason Aronson.

Hughes, D. (1998). *Building the Bonds of Attachment: Awakening Love in deeply Troubled Children*. Northvale, NJ: Jason Aronson

James, B. (1994). *Handbook for Treatment of Attachment-Trauma Problems in Children*. New York: Lexington.

Kagan, R. (2004). *Rebuilding Attachments with Traumatized Children: Healing from Losses, Violence, Abuse, and Neglect*. Binghamton, NY: The Haworth Press.

Levy, T. & Orlans, M. (1998). *Attachment, Trauma, and Healing*. Washington DC: CWLA.

Mahler, M., Pine, F., & Bergman, A. (1975). *The Psychological Birth of the Human Infant*. New York: Basic Books.

Pastzor, E.M., Leighton, M., & Blome, W.W. (1993). *Helping Children and Youths Develop Positive Attachments*. Washington, DC: Child Welfare League of America.

Real Life Heroes: Practitioner's Manual
Published by The Haworth Press, Inc., 2007. All rights reserved.
doi:10.1300/5639_21

Peterson, J. (1994). The Invisible Road; Parental Insights to Attachment Disorder. Self-Published Manu-
    script.
Schore, A. (1994). *Affect Regulation and the Origin of the Self: The Neurobiology of Emotional Devel-
    opment.* Hillsdale, NJ: Lawrence Erlbaum Associates.

Storytelling and Narrative Therapies

Bettelheim, B. (1975). *The Uses of Enchantment: The Meaning and Importance of Fairy Tales.* New
    York: Vintage Books.
Combs, G. & Freedman, J. (1990). *Symbol, Story, and Ceremony: Using Metaphor in Individual and
    Family Therapy.* New York: Norton.
Duhl, B. (1983). *From the Inside Out and Other Metaphors.* New York: Brunner/Mazel.
Evans, M.D. (1986). *This is Me and My Two Families.* New York: Magination Press.
Freedman, J. & Combs, G. (1996). *Narrative therapy; The social construction of preferred realities.*
    New York: Norton.
Gardner, R. (1975). *Psychotherapeutic Approaches to the Resistant Child.* New York: Jason Aronson.
Gardner, R. (1986). *Therapeutic Communication with Children.* Lanham, MD: Jason Aronson.
Jewett, C. (1978). *Adopting The Older Child.* Cambridge, MA: The Harvard Common Press. (See chap-
    ter on life stories.)
Kagan, R. (1982). Storytelling and game therapy for children in placement. *Childcare Quarterly, 11*(4),
    280-290.
Kagan, R. (2004). *Real Life Heroes: A Life Storybook for Children.* Binghamton, NY: The Haworth
    Press.
Lankton, C. & Lankton, S. (1989). *Tales of Enchantment.* New York: Brunner/Mazel.
Munson, L. & Riskin, K. (1995). *In Their Own Words: A Sexual Abuse Workbook for Teenage Girls.*
    Washington DC: Child Welfare League of America.
Roberts, J. (1994). *Tales and Transformations—Stories in Families and Family Therapy.* New York:
    Norton.
Suddaby, K. & Landau, J. (1998). Positive and negative timelines: A technique for restorying. *Family
    Process, 37* (3), 287-297.
Wheeler, C. (1978). *Where am I Going? Making a Child's Life Story Book.* Juneau, AK: The Winking
    Owl Press.
White, M. & Epston, D. (1990). *Narrative Means to Therapeutic Ends.* New York: Norton.

Trauma Therapies

Cloitre, M., Koenen, K.C., & Cohen, L. R. (2006). *Treating Survivors of Childhood Abuse: Psychother-
    apy for the Interrupted Life.* New York: Guilford.
Cohen, J.A., Deblinger, E., & Mannarino, A.P. (2006). *Treating Trauma and Traumatic Grief in Chil-
    dren and Adolescents.* New York: Guilford.
Deblinger, E. & Heflin, A.H. (1996). *Treating Sexually Abused Children and Their Non-Offending Par-
    ents: A Cognitive Behavioral Approach.* Thousand Oaks: Sage.
Figley, C. (1989). *Helping Traumatized Families.* San Francisco: Jossey-Bass.
Ford, J. D. & Russo, E. (2006). A trauma-focused, present-centered, emotional self-regulation approach
    to integrated treatment for post-traumatic stress and addiction: Trauma Adaptive Recovery Group Ed-
    ucation and Therapy (TARGET). *American Journal of Psychotherapy.* See also www.ptsdfreedom
    .org. for TARGET materials.
Gil, E. (1991). *The Healing Power of Play.* New York: Guilford.
Gil, E. (1996). *Treating Abused Adolescents.* New York: Guilford.
Greenwald, R. (1999). *Eye Movement Desensitization and Reprocessing (EMDR) in Child and
    Adolescent Psychotherapy.* Northvale, NJ: Jason Aronson.
James, B. (1989). *Treating Traumatized Children.* Lexington, MA: Lexington Books.
Kagan, R. (2004). *Rebuilding Attachments with Traumatized Children: Healing from Losses, Violence,
    Abuse, and Neglect.* Binghamton, NY: The Haworth Press.

Kolko, D. & Swenson, C.C. (2002). *Assessing and Treating Physically Abused Children and Their Families.* Thousand Oaks, CA: Sage.

Macy, R. D., Barry, S., & Gil, N.G. (2003). *Youth Facing Threat and Terror: Supporting Preparedness and Resilience.* San Francisco: Jossey-Bass.

Schore, A.N. (2003). Early relational trauma, disorganized attachment, and the development of a predisposition to violence. In Solomon, M.F. & Siegel, D.J. (Eds.), *Healing Trauma: Attachment, Mind, Body, and Brain.* New York: Norton.

Shapiro, F. (2001). *Eye Movement Desensitization and Reprocessing; Basic Principles, Protocols, and Procedures* (Second edition). New York: Guilford Press.

Shapiro, F. and Forrest, M.S. (1997). *EMDR: The Breakthrough Therapy for Overcoming Anxiety, Stress, and Trauma.* New York: Basic Books.

Siegel, D. (1999). *The Developing Mind.* New York: Guilford Press.

Siegel, D. (2003). An interpersonal neurobiology of psychotherapy: The developing mind and the resolution of trauma. In Solomon, M.F., & Siegel, D.J. (Eds.) *Healing Trauma: Attachment, Mind, Body, and Brain.* New York: Norton.

Tinker, R.H. & Wilson, S.A. (1998). *Through the Eyes of a Child: EMDR with Children.*

van der Kolk, B. (2003). Posttraumatic stress disorder and the nature of trauma. In Solomon, M.F. & Siegel, D.J. (Eds.), *Healing Trauma: Attachment, Mind, Body, and Brain.* New York: Norton.

van der Kolk, B.A., McFarlane, A.C., & Weisaeth, L. (eds.) (1996). *Traumatic Stress.* New York: Guilford Press.

Child and Family Services

Finkelstein, N.E. (1991). *Children and Youth in Limbo: A Search for Connections.* New York: Praeger.

Kagan, R. (1996). *Turmoil to Turning Points: Building Hope for Children in Crisis Placements.* New York: Norton.

Kagan, R. (2000). "My game," rebuilding hope for children in placement. In C. E. Schaefer & S. E. Reid (Eds.), *Game Play: Therapeutic Uses of Childhood Games.* New York: Wiley.

Kagan, R. & Schlosberg, S. (1989). *Families in Perpetual Crisis.* New York: Norton.

Kaplan, L. & Girard, J.L. (1994). *Strengthening High-Risk Families: A Handbook for Therapists.* New York: Lexington Books.

Klass, C.S. (1996). *Home Visiting.* Baltimore: Brookes.

Schorr L.B. (1998). *Common Purpose: Strengthening Families and Neighborhoods to Rebuild America.* Doubleday/Anchor.

Steinhauer, P. (1991) *The Least Detrimental Alternative: A Systematic Guide to Case Planning and Decision-making for Children in Care.* Toronto: University of Toronto Press.

Chapter 16

Heroes Library

Recommended books for children and adolescents listed by age, reading level, and challenges in their lives

Real Life Heroes: Practitioner's Manual
Published by The Haworth Press, Inc., 2007. All rights reserved.
doi:10.1300/5639_22

Title	Author	Subject	Reading Level	Description	Comments
The Little Engine That Could	Piper, Watty	Child hero story, overcoming obstacles	Preschool	A little train carrying oodles of toys to all the good boys and girls is confronted with a towering mountain. He overcomes and finds his way to the other side.	"models determination"
Goodnight Moon	Brown, Margaret Wise	Child fear	Preschool, Grades K-4	Child overcomes fears of dark by saying goodnight to everything.	"uses attention to details in a ritualized manner to create a feeling of safety at bedtime"
Today I Feel Silly	Curtis, Jaime Lee	Moods	Preschool, Grades K-4	This book takes the reader through 13 different moods, and helps explain mood swings to children.	N/A
It's My Body (Children's Safety and Abuse Prevention)	Freeman, Lory	Recognizing Sexual Abuse	Preschool, Grades K-4	Informative paperback that explains good and bad touch to children.	N/A
I Can't Talk About it: A Child's Book About Sexual Abuse (A Corner of the Heart)	Sanford, Doris	Talking about sexual abuse	Preschool, Grades K-4	Young girl reveals her sexual abuse to a dove who helps her heal and learn to trust again. The book also lists guideline for adults to help sexually abused children.	N/A
Horton Hatches the Egg	Dr. Seuss	Parenting	Preschool, Grades K-4	Horton is persuaded to sit on and hatch an egg while the mother takes a break.	"teaches the meaning of parenting"
Runaway Bunny	Brown, Margaret Wise	Child hero story	Grades K-4	A little rabbit who wants to runaway tells his mother how he will escape, but she is always right behind him.	"for a children who are interested in nature and animals"

Title	Author	Theme	Grade	Description	Notes
Stellaluna	Cannon, Jannell	Children's adversity story	Grades K-4	Story of a bat who overcomes separation, foster care, racial differences, and reuniting with mother.	
Alexander and the Terrible, Horrible, No Good Very Bad Day	Cruz, Ray	Overcoming adversity	Grades K-4	Story of Alexander's very bad day, and how he overcomes feeling horrible about it.	"is an engaging story of frustration with the lesson that some days are just like that"
Hansel and Gretel	Grimm, Jacob	Children's adversity story	Grades K-4	Clever children overcome fears and triumph over evil.	
Elephant in the Living Room: A Children's Book	Hastings, Jill M.	Child trauma, Substance abuse	Grades K-4	Children's story that uses an elephant to illustrate the experience having a relative in the house who is a substance abuser.	"demonstrates overcoming secrecy supporting addictions"
A Terrible Thing Happened: A Story for Children Who Have Witnessed Violence or Trauma	Holmes, Margaret M.	Trauma	Grades K-4	Story of Sherman who sees something terrible, and becomes anxious and angry. After seeing a counselor, he talks through emotions and feels better.	Young raccoon who sees something terrible happen and how it preoccupies him. His PTSD / anxiety changes his behavior, his parents send him to a therapist, and he overcomes this and moves on.
Little Red Riding Hood	Hyman, Trina	Children's adversity story	Grades K-4	Little Red Riding Hood lessons; Keeping promises, to stay on the path, mind her manners, and avoid talking to big bad wolves.	
Ray Charles	Mathis, Sharon Bell	Real life hero story	Grades K-4	Life story of Ray Charles, African American jazz musician without sight.	African American Musician who lost his sight at seven
There is a Nightmare in my Closet	Mayer, Mercer	Overcoming fears	Grades K-4	At bedtime a boy confronts the nightmare in his closet and finds him not so terrifying.	"a great example of a child mastering his fears"

Title	Author	Subject	Reading Level	Description	Comments
We Are All in the Dumps with Jack and Guy	Sendeck, Maurice	Child Hero / Overcoming adversity	Grades K-4	Sendak takes old nursery rhymes and illustrates hardships of today's world, and the life of orphans living on the streets that are being watched over by the moon. A headline from the book says it all "Leaner Times, Meaner Times, Children Triumph."	This book should be read by and an adult to the child to ad in discussion of the illustrations (which tell the story more so then the words?
Where the Wild Things Are	Sendak, Maurice	Child hero stories	Grades K-4	Story of Jack, who after mischief, is sent to his room. His room turns to a forest, where he meets a series of monsters, who are scary looking without being scary.	"about a defiant child's dream that incorporates becoming like monsters, starting a voyage (courage), and returning to the smell of a hot meal prepared by his mother (reunification)"
Double Fudge	Blume, Judy		Grades 4-6		
Freckle Juice	Blume, Judy		Grades 4-6		
The One in the Middle Is a Green Kangaroo	Blume, Judy		Grades 4-6		
Otherwise Known As Sheila the Great	Blume, Judy		Grades 4-6		
Tales of a Fourth Grade Nothing	Blume, Judy		Grades 4-6		
Mouse and the Motorcycle	Cleary, Beverley		Grades 4-6		
Muggie Maggie	Cleary, Beverley		Grades 4-6		

Title	Author	Theme	Grade	Description	Notes
Ramona Boxed Set	Cleary, Beverley	Child hero story, overcoming diversity	Grades 4-6	Four stories of Ramona learning life lessons, including: being patient with her sister, her first crush, staying out of trouble, learning bravery, overcoming fears, gaining maturity, and meeting expectations.	
Runaway	Cleary, Beverley		Grades 4-6		
James and the Giant Peach	Dahl, Roald	Child Hero / Overcoming adversity	Grades 4-6	James loses his parents, and is forced to live with his wicked and abusive aunts. He become the saddest and loneliest boy you could find. He meets a man who gives him magic crystals that fall onto his aunts peach tree. The tree develops a peach of enormous proportions and he climbs inside, where he finds and assortment of characters who help him through his pain.	Also made in to a motion picture. This is a great book for children who feel abandoned or neglected by their parents. It also helps aid in coping with the death of a parent.
Matilda	Dahl, Roald	Child Hero, overcoming abuse	Grades 4-6		
Revolting Rhymes	Dahl, Roald		Grades 4-6		
Joey Pigza Loses Control	Gantos, Jack	ADD, overcoming diversity	Grades 4-6	Joey wants six-week visit with father to count and show him that he can control his ADD. His father makes up for past wrongs, and shows Joey how to be a winner and take control of his life.	

Title	Author	Subject	Reading Level	Description	Comments
Joey Pigza Swallowed the Key	Gantos, Jack	ADD, overcoming di-versity	Grades 4-6	Joey cannot sit still, can't pay attention, can't follow rules, and can't help it. He was born with ADD. He wreaks havoc on class trips and swallows his house key. Joey knows he is a good kid, and no matter how hard he tries to do the right thing, everything goes wrong.	
What Would Joey do?	Gantos, Jack	ADD, divorce, over-coming diversity	Grades 4-6	Joey learns that settling down isn't good for anything if he can't find a way to stop the people he cares about from winding him up all over again.	
Odds on Oliver	Green, Constance C.	Child Hero	Grades 4-6	Oliver, desperate to be a hero, after many attempts and failures, triumphs when held hostage in a grocery store and finds the solution to get out.	
The Best of Girls to the Rescue	Lansky, Bruce - edt.	overcoming diversity, child hero story	Grades 4-6	Girls featured in the *Girls to the Rescue* series are smart, and save the day	
The New Captain Under-pants Collection: Box Set (books 1 - 5)	Pilkey, Dav	Hero Stories	Grades 4-6	Five books with stories of Captain Underpants and his adventures.	After working in the library for several years, I found these books almost never stayed on the shelves. They are funny, and kids love them. They also have a hero figure who concurs many obstacles.

Title	Author	Genre / Type	Grade	Description
Shiloh	Reynolds, Phyllis		Grades 4-6	Boy befriends abused dog.
Holes	Sacher, Louis	Child hero story	Grades 4-6	teaches kids to persevere and builds confidence
Marvin Redpost: Alone in His Teachers House	Sacher, Louis		Grades 4-6	
Sideways Stories from Wayside School	Sacher, Louis		Grades 4-6	
Sixth Grade Secrets	Sacher, Louis		Grades 4-6	
Falling Up	Silverstein, Shel		Grades 4-6	
A Light in the Attack	Silverstein, Shel		Grades 4-6	
Where the Sidewalk Ends	Silverstein, Shel	Children's Poetry	Grades 4-6	
Hatchet	Paulsen, Gary	Child hero stories / Overcoming adversity	Grades 7-10	After a plane crash, thirteen-year-old Brian spends fifty-four days in the wilderness with only a hatchet to survive. He is also learning to deal with his parents' divorce. "a boy who crash lands and must learn to survive in the wilderness"
The Children's Homer: The Adventures of Odysseus and the Tale of Troy	Colum, Padraic	Hero / Mythology	YA	Book tells the story of Odysseus and his adventures in Troy as well as his journey home to his wife and kingdom. A classic epic of a journey through hardships and obstacles to achieve goals.

Title	Author	Subject	Reading Level	Description	Comments
Freak the Mighty	Philbrick, Rodman	Child Hero	YA	Story of two boys that do not fit the norm, and are outcast by peers. One for being big and having a criminal father, the other due to crippling illness. They befriend each other, and make Freak the Mighty, more powerful together then alone. Together they face adventure, and danger. In the end, Mighty, copes with the death of Freak, and learns a powerful lesson about himself.	Wonderful book for children with differences that may make them feel they accepted by their peers. It encourages education, reading and imagination to triumph through it. Made into a motion picture called *The Mighty*.
Big Fish: A Novel of Mythic Proportions	Wallace, Danielle	Modern Myth / Hero Story / Father and son relationship	YA	Edward Bloom (Big Fish) and son go through epic story of father's life. Edward spent his life exploring and telling jokes, and stories. Son tries to connect with father during the last moments of his life, and understands who the man is behind the myth.	Also made into a motion picture in 2004
Autobiography of Malcolm X	X, Malcolm	Real life hero story	YA	Story of Malcolm X's life.	
Object Lessons	Quindlen, Anna	Coming of age	YA, Grades 7-10 and up	Child's struggle with her identity and her mother's mistakes.	"For adolescents grappling with their parents' strengths and mistakes"

Title	Author	Category	Level	Description
Harry Potter Hardcover Box Set with Leather Bookmark (books 1-5)	Rowling, J.K.	Child Hero	YA, Grades 7-10 and up	Story of orphaned boy living with abusive relatives, discovers his magical powers (inherited from his parents) and goes off to school to develop them. While there he has a series of adventures that uncover more of his powers and give him a deeper insight into self. Kids love these books (as do adults)
Malcolm X: By any Means Necessary: A Biography	Myers, Walter Dean	Real life hero story	Juvenile Non-fiction	Life story of Malcolm X's life.
Please Tell: A Child's Story About Sexual Abuse	Ottenweler, Jessie	Child Hero, Overcoming sexual abuse	Juvenile Non-fiction, Ages 4-8	Life Story and illustrations of nine-year-old Jessie to help let other sexually abused child its okay to talk about their feelings.
Bury My Heart at Wounded Knee: An Indian History of the American West	Brown, Dee Alexander	Real life hero story	Juvenile Non-fiction, Grade 4-6	Life story of Sioux Indians at Wounded Knee in S. Dakota. It tells how Indians lost their lives and land to white society and how they endured the suffering of their people and the abolishing of their cultures and community. Native American perspective of American History
A Boy Called Slow: The True Story of Sitting Bull	Bruchac, Joseph	Real life hero story	Juvenile Non-fiction, Grades 4-6	Life story of Sitting Bull, Lakota Sioux Indian.
The Leroy Butler Story... From Wheelchair to the Lamseau Leap	Butler, Leroy	Real life hero story	Juvenile Non-fiction, Grade 4-6	Tells the story of Leroy Butler, former Green Bay Packer, overcoming childhood health problems and moving onto college and becoming a football hero; eventually winning Super bowl XXXI.

Title	Author	Subject	Reading Level	Description	Comments
Go Free or Die: A Story About Harriet Tubman	Ferris, Jeri	Real life hero story	Juvenile nonfiction, Grade 4-6	Life story of Harriet Tubman and her role in helping slaves escape bondage.	
Brave Bessie: Flying Free	Fisher, Lillian M.	Real life hero story	Juvenile nonfiction, Grades 4-6	Life story of Bessie Smith, African-American female aviator.	Two years before Amelia Earhart, Bessie Smith became the first African American aviatrix to receive her flying license
Brother Eagle, Sister Sky: A Message from Chief Seattle	Jeffers, Susan	Real life hero story	Juvenile nonfiction, Grades 4-6	Adaptation of a speech given by Chief Seattle at treaty negations in the 1850s.	
A School for Pompey Walker	Rosen, Michael J.	Real life hero story	Juvenile nonfiction, Graded 4-6	Inspired by the true story of a young freed slave, who with the help of a white man, sells himself back into slavery thirty-nine times to raise money for school.	Story of Gussie West
When Justice Failed: The Fred Korematsu Story (Stories of America)	Tamura, David	Real life hero story	Juvenile nonfiction, Grades 4-6	Story of Fred Korematsu, born in California, volunteered for military service but rejected because of Japanese ancestry. Book covers his battle with supreme court after refusing to leave his home to live in internment camp.	
Kids Write Through It		Children's adversity story	Juvenile nonfiction, Grades 4-6, and 7-10	Kids ages seven to twelve write about overcoming their challenges on a variety of issues including mental illness and death.	Stories by kids, for kids

Title	Author	Theme/Type	Level	Description
Kids with Courage: True Stories of Young People Making a Difference	Barbara A. Lewis	Child hero stories	YA nonfiction, Grades 7-10	Eighteen young people respond to heroically overcoming crises in their lives.
I Know Why the Caged Bird Sings	Maya Angelou	Real life hero story	YA nonfiction, Grades 7-10 and up	Life story of Maya Angelou and her struggles to overcome abusive childhood.
A Child Called "It"	Dave Pelzer	Real life hero story, overcoming adversity and trauma	YA, Adult nonfiction, Grade 7-10 and up	Life story of Dave Pelzer and his overcoming of childhood abuse. Part of series of four books; *A Child Called "It"* and its sequel to expand a youth's understanding and perspective of how people survive and grow despite neglect, violence or abuse.

Movies

Title	Author	Theme/Type	Level	Description
Finding Forrester		Child hero story, overcoming obstacles, caring adult	Adolescent	Young gifted black male befriends sick introverted author and develops his writing talents.
Finding Nemo		Child hero story, overcoming obstacles	Ages 10 and up	Young Nemo, defiant to fathers overbearing paranoia, accidentally gets caught and put into a dentist's fish tank. Father, faces his own fears to find his son. During his journey he meets others who help him along the way, and help him further overcome his paranoia.

Title	Author	Subject	Reading Level	Description	Comments
The Land Before Time		Child hero story, overcoming obstacles	Ages 4 and up	Orphaned dinosaur has to make his way to the great valley in order to survive a plague. Along the way, he meets up with others from all different dinosaur species. They bond and travel together, finding ways to deal with the obstacles that lay in their path.	
Lilo and Stitch		Family / Foster care, child hero story	Ages 5 and up	Story teaches that a family can be assembled or born into.	
Shiloh					
Shrek		Hero story, Epic adventure	Ages 5 and up	Shrek, misunderstood ogre, makes a deal with the king to rescue Princess to get his land back. During this excursion, Shrek learns to make friends, fall in love, and overcomes many obstacles to achieve his goal.	
Star Wars Trilogy		Hero story, Epic adventure	Adolescent	Luke Skywalker, Jedi warrior, struggles to discover his Jedi powers, find his father, and defeat the dark side.	"in which an orphaned hero, Luke, is guided by his uncle, Obi Wan, to calm, center himself, and develop his skills, and elicit powers to help others"
Whale Rider		Overcoming diversity	Adolescent	Legend of Paikea overcoming diversity she faces being a girl trying to lead the Maori tribe in New Zealand.	

Title	Author/Source	Theme	Audience	Description
What's Eating Gilbert Grape	based on a novel by Peter Hedges	Over coming diversity, families and mental illness	Caring adult	Gilbert handles running the family, caring for brother with mental disabilities, caring for obese bed-ridden mother and death in family. He eventually breaks free, and finds a new role in life.
White Oleander		Neglectful parents, foster care	Adult	Story of abuse, and a child growing up in foster care.

Music

Title	Author	Audience	Description	Notes
Follow Me	Uncle Cracker	6 and up	Caring person	
Hero	Mariah Carey	6 and up		
I Will Survive	Gloria Gaynor	Adolescent	Overcoming hardships	
I'll be There	Mariah Carey	6 and up	Caring person	
I'm Beautiful	Christina Aguilera	6 and up	Overcoming taunts	
One	U2	6 and up	Overcoming pain	This song is about finding love for others, even through differences, to help "carry each other" through the pains in life
Wind Beneath My Wings	Bette Midler	6 and up	Caring person, hero song	
You've Got a Friend	James Taylor	Adolescent		

Chapter 17

Developmental-, Trauma-, and Attachment-Centered Service Planning

Worksheets and Summary

ATTACHMENT ECOGRAM

Family Name: _____

First Names: _____ ; _____ ; _____

Dates of Assessment: _____ ; _____ ; _____

Dates of Birth: _____ ; _____ ; _____

Ages: _____ ; _____ ; _____

Referred by: _____

For Court: Yes/No   Needed by: _____

Reasons for Referral

_____

_____

_____

_____

Ecogram

Community
Resources

Key: Linkage Symbols

- – – Tentative or partial support, past or present
- ——— Adult believes, nurtures, and protects child in the present
- ═══ Adult committed to nurturing and protecting child until maturity

Real Life Heroes: Practitioner's Manual
Published by The Haworth Press, Inc., 2007. All rights reserved.
doi:10.1300/5639_23

Metaphors (Striking Behaviors, Key Words)

_____

_____

_____

_____

Community Resources

_____

_____

_____

_____

Initial Evaluation

Child   Strengths/Problems

_____   _____

_____   _____

_____   _____

_____   _____

_____   _____

_____   _____

_____   _____

Time Line

Age   Date   Significant Events, Lived with, Services

_____   _____   _____

_____   _____   _____

_____   _____   _____

_____   _____   _____

_____   _____   _____

_____   _____   _____

_____   _____   _____

_____   _____   _____

_____   _____   _____

_____   _____   _____

_____   _____   _____

_____   _____   _____

_____   _____   _____

_____   _____   _____

_____   _____   _____

_____   _____   _____

PREVIOUS EVALUATIONS/NOTES: _____

_____

_____

_____

_____

_____

_____

_____

_____

_____

_____

_____

_____

_____

_____

_____

_____

_____

_____

_____

Youth/Family: _____ Age: _____ Dates: _/_/_; _/_/_; _/_/_; _/_/_; Needed: _/_/_

Reasons for Referral/Placement: _____

Permanency Plan: (1.) _____ (2.) _____ Planned Discharge: _/_/_

TRAUMA-ATTACHMENT ASSESEMENT

Behavior/Dress/Key Words _____

Developmental Age: Emotional __; Social __; Reasoning __; Verbal Expressive __;
Reading __; Fine Motor __; Gross Motor __

Strengths (Youth/Family/Cultural/Spiritual): _____

_____

Problems: _____

_____

Youth Goals: _____ Parent/Guardian Goals: _____

Primary Attachments: _____

Supportive Family/Mentors: _____

Losses: _____

Traumas: _____

_____

Misperceptions: _____

Negative Beliefs: _____

_____

Positive Beliefs: _____

_____

Affect Recognition: (1-10) __; Affect Regulation: (1-10) __; Impulse Control: (1-10) __

Triggers: _____

Traumatic Stress Reactions: _____

_____

Primary risks: ❑ Harm to self ❑ Harm to others ❑ Drug/Alcoohol ❑ Dissociation
❑ Other _____

❑ With family: _____

❑ With peers: _____

❑ With therapists/caring adults: _____

_____

_____

_____

SERVICE PLANNING

Evaluations: ❑ Psychological   ❑ Drug/Alcohol   ❑ Medical/Neurological/Psychotropic

❑ Coordinate with: _____   ❑ Info. from: _____

❑ Validation/Safety by: _____; _____; _____   ❑ Nurture-Guidance
by: _____; _____; _____; ❑ Mentors: _____; _____

❑ Contract for Conferences/Monitoring/Safety plans with: _____

❑ Safety Plans for Risks/Triggers (When/Where/How/By Whom): _____

_____

_____

_____

❑ Trauma-Attachment Focus: _____

Youth Skillbuilding

❑ Affect Reg.   ❑ Social   ❑ Problem Solving   ❑ Trauma Psychoed.

❑ Beliefs   ❑ Threat Avoidance   ❑ Concentration   ❑ Memory   ❑ Triggers

❑ Relapse Prevention   ❑ Life Story   ❑ Cultural/Family Heritage   ❑ Spirituality

❑ Aerobic Exercise   ❑ Art   ❑ Music   ❑ Dance   ❑ Sports   ❑ Other _____

❑ Education   ❑ Reading   ❑ Math   ❑ Writing   ❑ Test taking   ❑ Vocational _____

❑ Activities/Skills/Talents: _____

❑ Mentoring/Tutoring: _____; ❑ Helping Others by: _____

Parent/Guardian Skillbuilding

❑ Affect Reg.   ❑ Nurture   ❑ Dev'l Expectations

❑ Discipline   ❑ Validation   ❑ Domestic Violence (Recognition, Protection)

❑ Relapse Prevention   ❑ Other _____

Legal: ❑ ASFA timeline   ❑ Petitions/letters to court/law guardian/CASA)

ASSESSMENT AND SERVICE SUMMARY

Name: _____ **Age:** _____ **Date:** _____

1. Developmental age: emotional __; social __; reasoning/comprehension __

2. Traumatic stress: losses __, domestic violence __, neglect __, physical abuse __, sexual abuse __, medical trauma __, community violence __? What happened at what age?

_____

_____

_____

_____

_____

_____

3. Attachments: validation/safety by: _____; _____; _____;

   nurture-guidance by: _____; _____; _____;

   mentors: _____; _____; _____; potential: _____

   Primary attachments of the child: __ Secure __ Insecure-Anxious __ Insecure-Avoidant __ Chaotic-Disorganized __ On-attached

4. Strengths (skills; talents; caring, supportive adults, siblings, & relatives; cultural, spirituality)? _____

_____

_____

_____

_____

_____

   Child's Affect Regulation (1-10): __ Impulse Control (1-10): __
   Parent-Guardian's Affect Regulation (1-10): __ Impulse Control (1-10): __

5. "Triggers" to traumatic stress (child, family, school, community) and reactions (problems)

_____

_____

_____

_____

_____

_____

Child's Stress (1-10): __   Primary Parent-Guardian's Stress (1-10): __

Risks: ❑ Self-harm ❑ Suicidal ❑ Harm to others ❑ Drugs/Alcohol ❑ Dissociation
           ❑ Other _____

Service Plan

1. Safety plans for known risks and triggers to trauma reactions (Trigger/Risk Signs/Who will do what for each location): _____

_____

_____

_____

_____

_____

_____

_____

2. Building/rebuilding committed caring relationships and attachments with:

    1. _____ 2. _____ 3. _____ 4. _____

3a. Child skill building:

    ❑ Affect Regulation ❑ Social ❑ Problem Solving ❑ Threat Avoidance

    ❑ Concentration ❑ Memory ❑ Triggers ❑ Relapse Prevention _____

Education: ❑ Reading ❑ Math ❑ Writing ❑ Test taking ❑ Vocational

❑ Activities/Skills/Talents: _____

b. Parent/guardian skill-building:

❑ Affect Regulation ❑ Nurture ❑ Developmental Expectations ❑ Discipline

❑ Validation of child ❑ Domestic Violence (Recognition, Protection)

❑ Relapse Prevention

4. Trauma reintegration:

❑ Trauma Psychoeducation ❑ Dysfunctional Beliefs ❑ Triggers

❑ Desensitization ❑ Life Story—Creating a new future

Modalities: ❑ Art ❑ Music ❑ Movement/Dance ❑ Sports ❑ Spirituality

5. Community reintegration:

❑ Family ❑ School ❑ Mentors ❑ Helping others

Chapter 18

Important People Questionnaire

Name:_____ **Date:**_____

Please think about people in your life and write in their names.

When you were little:

Who helped you at age three or four, when you were sick? _____

Who helped you at age three or four, if you were scared at night? _____

Who helped you with homework in first grade? _____

Who taught you to ride a bike? _____

Who showed they appreciated what you had done, for instance, a great basketball shot, a good report card, a great painting in school? _____

Now that you are older:

If you were given $3,000 and a one-week vacation, what would you do? _____

_____

Who would you most like to spend your vacation with? _____

Who will really listen to you when you need to talk to someone? _____

Who can you count on to help you in a crisis? _____

Who would tell you when you are wrong and help you make things better? _____

Real Life Heroes: Practitioner's Manual
Published by The Haworth Press, Inc., 2007. All rights reserved.
doi:10.1300/5639_24

These are the people I care the most about: _____

_____

Who have you helped? _____

Five years from now:

Who could you look to for help in a crisis? _____

Who would believe in you? _____

Who would you like to be your friend? _____

Who would tell you when you are wrong and help you make things better? _____

Who would you like to help? _____

Just a few more questions:

1. How many people can you think of who cared about you *and* helped you from the time you were a baby to your present age? Please circle the closest answer:

   0   1   2   3   4   5-7   8-10   11-15   16-20   20-30   30+

2. When you think about your life, from the time you were a baby until today, how do you feel? Please circle the number that best shows how you feel:

   0   1   2   3   4   5   6   7   8   9   10
   (peaceful)   (upset)

3. When you think about your life, from the time you were a baby until today, how do you think about yourself. Please circle the number that best shows how you would describe yourself:

   0   1   2   3   4   5   6   7   8   9   10
   (terrible)   (good)

4. At your present age, how many people can you think of who care about you *and* would help you if you were in serious trouble? Please circle the closest answer:

   0   1   2   3   4   5-7   8-10   11-15   16-20   20-30   30+

What do you think would help make things better for you and the people you care about the most?

_____

_____

_____

_____

_____

_____

_____

_____

_____

Thank you for completing this form!

Chapter 19

My Thermometers: Self-Monitoring

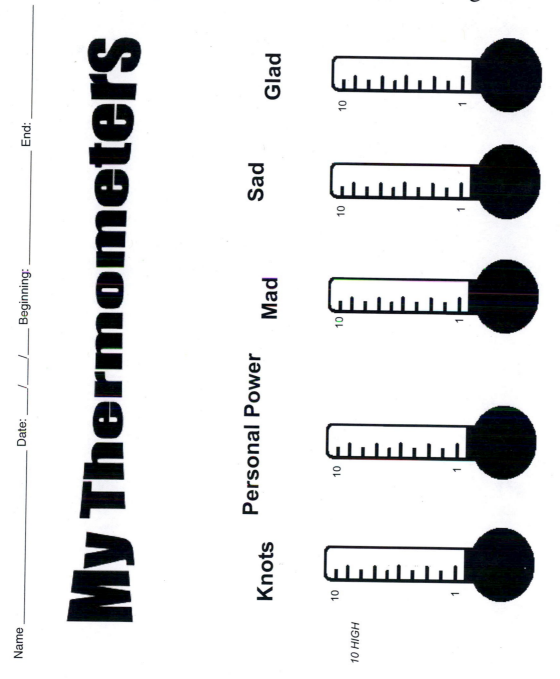

Name _____

Date: _____ / _____ / _____   Beginning: _____   End: _____

My Thermometers

Glad 10 1

Sad 10 1

Mad 10 1

Personal Power 10 1

Knots 10 1

10 HIGH

Real Life Heroes: Practitioner's Manual
Published by The Haworth Press, Inc., 2007. All rights reserved.
doi:10.1300/5639_25

Chapter 20

Stronger and Stronger
Progress Chart

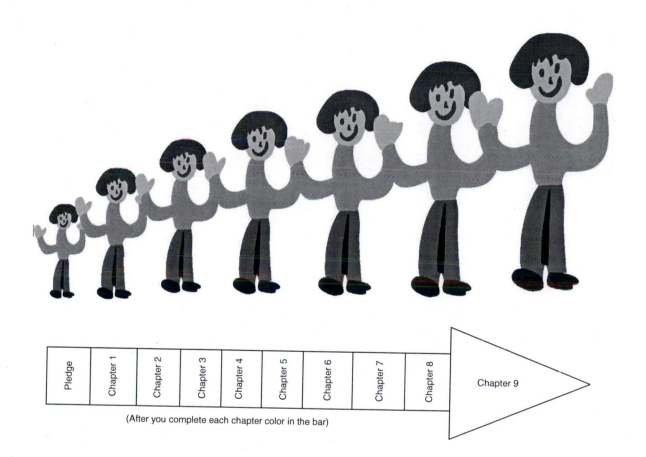

| Pledge | Chapter 1 | Chapter 2 | Chapter 3 | Chapter 4 | Chapter 5 | Chapter 6 | Chapter 7 | Chapter 8 | Chapter 9 |

(After you complete each chapter color in the bar)

Real Life Heroes: Practitioner's Manual
Published by The Haworth Press, Inc., 2007. All rights reserved.
doi:10.1300/5639_26

Chapter 21

Session Summary/Progress Notes

Child: _____ Date: _____

Adults participating in session: _____

Check off (✓):

❑ Self-Check Thermometers (1-10): *Knots:* _____ *Personal Power:* _____ *Mad:* _____ *Sad:* _____ *Glad:* _____

❑ Safety First: safety plans in place; before/during/after reminders for predictable crises; child's signal and action plan if *Knots* begin to rise or *Personal Power* falls; plan for therapist self-care

❑ Openings: Magical Moment: e.g., herbal tea, cookie, magic trick, skills, special rituals, focusing/centering: deep breathing, imagery, balancing, humming, bubbles

❑ Chapter (circled) and pages completed: Pledge/Orientation 1 2 3 4 5 6 7 8 9 Notes/Narrative; pp: _____ — _____

1st: Nonverbally, select color, sketch image, tap rhythm, try out tone to match, then two to three note (chord improv), enact *Action Pose*

2nd: Invite child's thoughts on drawing, rhythm, music, and *Action Pose* and ask for verbal responses to questions listed on workbook page

3rd: Highlight strengths, coping skills, and positive beliefs about child growing in strength as child shares hardships and grieves losses and challenge dysfunctional beliefs

4th: Invite child to develop a story utilizing different modalities (music, art, movement) or to add photographs, video, or collages

❑ Repeat Self-Check Thermometers (1-10): *Knots:* _____ *Personal Power:* _____ *Mad:* _____ *Sad:* _____ *Glad:* _____

❑ Repeat Focusing/Centering exercises if necessary

❑ If possible, share child's work with safe, caring adult in session, or at another time, using tape recording of music, and drawings; encourage attunement by adult and validation of losses, hardships, adult responsibilities

❑ Reassurance: thoughts or feelings to be expected as normal; how your mind is healing and becoming stronger and stronger; how to utilize bodily sensations as messages or reminders; ways to calm and self-soothe using understanding of trauma and positive self-statements; choices; caring adults to call if distressed (on safety cards); plans with caring adults and children to manage reminders of traumas

Real Life Heroes: Practitioner's Manual
Published by The Haworth Press, Inc., 2007. All rights reserved.
doi:10.1300/5639_27

❏ End session on a positive note reinforcing strengths, lessons learned, helping others, etc.

❏ Homework: daily practice of self-soothing skills, safe, fun, and relationship-building activities.

Primary issues addressed:

_____

_____

_____

_____

_____

_____

_____

Triggers for Trauma Reactions:	Safety Plans (before/during/after):

Dysfunctional Beliefs and Toxic Memories:	Constructive Beliefs and Positive Memories:

Date set for next session: ___ / ___ / ___   Time: _____   Adults to invite: _____

Plans for Next Session:

_____

_____

_____

_____

_____

_____

_____

_____

_____

_____

_____

_____

Therapist: _____   Date: ____/____/____

Chapter 22

Bookmark

REAL LIFE HEROES
REMINDERS

* *Knots and Personal Power Thermometers*

* *Safety First*

* Openings: *Magical Moments* and Centering

* Page by Page, Stronger and Stronger

    Sketch
    Tap rhythm
    Add 2-3 note chord
    Try out *action pose*
    Answer questions

* Highlight strengths

* If desired, develop into story with beginning, middle, and end

* Repeat *Thermometers* and Centering

* When possible, share with safe adult

* Homework: Natural reactions and extra activities

* Time/date for next session

Real Life Heroes: Practitioner's Manual
Published by The Haworth Press, Inc., 2007. All rights reserved.
doi:10.1300/5639_28

Chapter 23

Traumatic Stress and the Hero's Challenge (Part I)

TRAUMATIC STRESS

Tough times start the alarm bells ringing in our bodies. That's a good thing. We feel our stomachs get tighter, our hearts beating faster, our arms and legs get ready for action. These are like little **Knots**[1] that wake us up to start thinking and do something to solve a problem.

Power for heroes means using our whole selves, our whole bodies from the tip of our toes to the thinking power of our brains. Power means self-awareness and self-control, and the ability to use our strength to reach our goals. We call it **Personal Power**[2] because it's ours, but only if we want to own it and use it. Personal Power is a skill, just like learning to ride a bike or shoot a basket, a skill we can

Real Life Heroes: Practitioner's Manual
Published by The Haworth Press, Inc., 2007. All rights reserved.
doi:10.1300/5639_29

grow stronger and stronger, as strong as the alarm bells that warn us of danger.

When we have Personal Power, we know when we are feeling worried but we also know we can think and plan and solve problems. We are in control. We also know we can get help from safe, caring adults and friends. With **Personal Power,** we can help ourselves and the people we care about.

But, sometimes the **tough times** are so horrible that our stomachs may start to ache. Our hearts feel like drums beating faster and faster until they feel like they might explode; and our arms and legs feel so tight they may burn. We may feel stuck, helpless, no good, or terrified. Things may seem especially horrible when **tough times** keep happening over and over. Our heads may hurt and everybody and everything may seem unfair and rotten. That's when our **Knots** may grow bigger than our **Personal Power.** The Alarm bell seems to

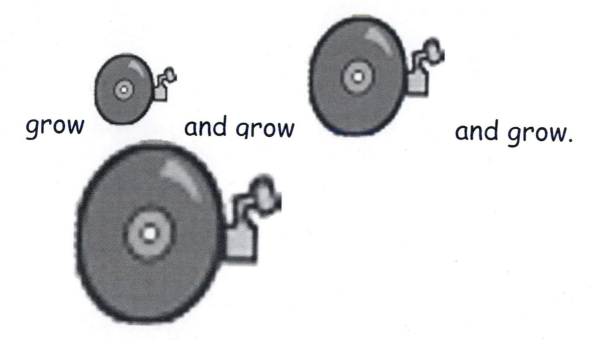

grow   and grow   and grow.

And, that's when it's easy to "blow your top,"

"lose your mind," and "get in trouble," even when you don't want to. It may feel like you can't turn the alarm off, or the bad memories about what happened, things that may seem too hard to say out loud. And, the only thing

you can think to do is to run away, or if

that doesn't work to hit, kick, fight

someone, or just freeze and try to

forget about everything and everybody.

That's traumatic stress.

FREEDOM

Heroes know that being hurt is part of real life. Bad things do happen. Sometimes good people get sick or get hurt or lose people they love. Heroes fight for FREEDOM to make sure that the bad times don't take over what is good in our lives, so we don't have to live with traumatic stress. Heroes use their skills to think and act, so they can make the world a little better for everyone, even when **tough times** seem horrible and impossible to change. Heroes don't stop thinking of a way to make things better and they stop traumatic stress from taking over.

You can do the same thing if you learn how to use F R E E D O M^3 to DEFEAT TRAUMAS and stay in control, even when **tough times** happen:

Focus: slow down, take a deep breath, check how you are feeling all over your body, look around for people, places, and things that make you feel safe. Check your legs, your arms, and your forehead so you know your **Knots. After all, it's your body.** Then, remember things that you can do and check your **Personal Power**.

Recognize your "Triggers": the people, places, and things that remind you of your tough times and start your alarm bell ringing.

Emotions: how do you really feel? Those are clues heroes use to solve problems.

Evaluate your thoughts: what do you really think about yourself and what can you do to make things better.

Define what is most important, your true goals.

Options: what can you do to reach one of your goals with help from friends, your family, and adults who are safe and care about you.[4]

M

ake the world a little bit better: what can you do, even just a little thing to help somebody else.

★ ★ ★ ★ ★

Now comes the hard part. Saying it, even writing it down, isn't enough. You have to do it.

And, just like learning to make a winning jump shot or play a guitar, it takes practice. And, sometimes, the more **tough times** you've had, the more practice and help you need. It's like learning to ride a bike, or shoot a bas-ket. At first, to a little child, it seems very hard. And, even a strong boy or girl may fail if they feel stressed. But then, with a lot of practice and a helpful guide, it suddenly clicks. You can do it.

The first step is to learn how to focus yourself so you are in control. This helps you grow your **Personal Power.** To do that, practice "SOS:"[5]

Slow Down: One thought at a time; breathe in and out, slower and slower, deeper and deeper. Fill up your whole body from the tip of your toes to the top of your head . . .

Orient Yourself: Focus on "right now," in this place; wiggle your toes. Listen to your breathing. Notice who's around who could help you. Look for people you like and calming objects or you can see or feel . . .

Self Check: Slowly scan over your body from the tip of your toes through your feet, ankles, knees, thighs, hips, stomach, chest, arms, and up your neck to your mouth, and all over your head to the very top. Rate yourself knots, your personal power, and how mad, sad, and glad you feel on My Thermometers or just a piece of paper.

Heroes know that staying calm and in control is a skill that can be learned with practice. It's very much like learning to ride a bike. It may seem hard, or even impossible at first, but then, with a lot of practice, it becomes easy.

To build your skills to calm down, even in **tough times,** try these steps for each of your five senses:[6]

Eyes: Look at a photograph of someone or something that makes you feel peaceful. Look at plants or flowers. Find something in every room and every place you go, that makes you feel good inside . . .

Ears: Listen to relaxing music, or even the music in a favorite person's voice. Sing along with a 'feel good' song. Tap a rhythm or play a an instrument. . .

Taste buds: Treat yourself to a tasty, soothing drink (e.g., hot chocolate or herbal tea). Sip slowly, as slowly as you can, and discover how good it tastes . . .

Nose: Sniff as you sip or pull out your favorite perfume. Sniff flowers, a spice, or a favorite treat . . .

Touch: Smooth a rich peaceful smelling lotion on your hand. Take a warm bubble bath, pet a friendly animal, rub a soft piece of fabric . . .

Now, add some action:

Take a walk.

Swim, play a sport, or exercise.

Learn and practice yoga or deep belly
    breathing.

Don't forget to get help from someone you trust:

Talk to a friend.

Hug someone.

To remember these steps, write your favorites down on a
card as part of your safety plan and put the card in your
wallet, backpack, or pocket along with names and phone
numbers of people you can call for help.

SAFETY FIRST

Five Senses Self-Soothing Plan:

Eyes: _____

Ears: _____

Taste buds: _____

Nose: _____

Touch: _____

Action Plan to Relax:

_____

_____

People I can call for help:

Police:

Teacher/Principal: _____   _____

_____   _____

Adults I trust: _____   _____

_____   _____

_____   _____

Friends I trust: _____   _____

_____   _____

_____   _____

Keep practicing your skill to calm down all five senses and to "SOS." The Workbook will also give you ways you can find people to help you, people you can help, and other ways to win your FREEDOM from traumatic stress. Step by step, chapter by chapter, you can take on the Hero's Challenge.

THE HERO'S CHALLENGE

It's hard to face traumatic stress. In many ways, it may seem easier to stay feeling trapped or stuck, not daring to change. Heroes muster the courage to heal from their wounds and use what they learn to help other people who have to face tough times.

Healing means using the pain in our lives to grow stronger.

Emotions are natural. Use them to grow smarter and stronger. Release the power of your own thinking.

Release the power of your own thinking.

Open Up Your Options.

Experiment: Muster the courage to check out and test out new solutions.

Stronger and **S**tronger: Find your skills and make them even stronger. Remember who cared about you in the past and find people who care enough to help you grow.

If you are ready to work on the Hero's Challenge, it's time to go to Chapter 3 of your **Real Life Heroes** book. . . . . . .

NOTES

1. Sutton, P. (2003). (2003). Personal communication.

2. Purdy, M. (2003). Personal communication.

3. Ford, J. D. & Russo, E. (2006). (Components of FREEDOM adapted from: A trauma-focused, present-centered, emotional self-regulation approach to integrated treatment for post-traumatic stress and addiction: Trauma adaptive recovery group education and therapy [TARGET]. *American Journal of Psychotherapy.*

4. Bloom, S. (1997). *Creating sanctuary: Toward the evolution of sane societies.* New York: Routledge.

5. Ford & Russo (2006).

6. Mahoney, K., Ford, J. D., & Cruz, St. Juste M. C. (2005). TARGET-A: *Trauma Adaptive Recovery Group Education and Therapy (10+ Session Adolescent Version) Racilitator Guide.* Farmington, CT: University of Connecticut Health Center.

Chapter 24

The ABCs of Trauma
and The Hero's Challenge
(Part II)

Tough times can make you feel like it's all your fault. Or, that nothing can change.

Here's how an "A" for "Action" can turn into an "F" for "Failing" faster than you can say A, B, C:

Action—Sometimes bad things happen that make us feel all knotted up inside like a close friend getting hurt badly in a football game after you tackled him or if you heard your mom and dad screaming at each other, getting into another fight, a door slamming and someone leaving, or, hearing someone you love has a terrible illness and may die. Later, your mom complains that your room is a mess again and you didn't do what she asked. Her face looks angry. That's when, *Action* can turn into *Alarm*. It's like your school's emergency alarm bell is going off inside in your body. You may be the only one who knows what happened. Then, the next day at school, a teacher looks angry and blames you for something you didn't do.

Real Life Heroes: Practitioner's Manual
Published by The Haworth Press, Inc., 2007. All rights reserved.
doi:10.1300/5639_30

Body reaction—Your brain's self-defense system kicks in. It's battle time. Your heart is pounding. Your fists clench. Your stomach is one giant knot. The alarm bell has grown louder and louder and you can't turn it off.[1] Before you know it, you slam your fist on your desk and start yelling at your teacher.

Catastrophic thinking—Your brain starts spinning: "That teacher hates me." "School stinks!" "Everybody is unfair to me."

Distress—Fear, rage, shock shut down your power to think, to figure things out. It's fight time.

Emptiness—Afterward, it's like: "Nobody cares." "I'm all alone." "No one can help me." "They think I'm no good." "Maybe I am really 'no good.'" Your stomach may ache. Your head may feel like it is spinning. You may feel you don't have much air in your chest. Your body starts slumping down . . .

Failing—Everyone seems to be looking at you. You see another "F" on the quiz your teacher puts on your desk. Or, you look down and see your desk is knocked over. Your teacher tells you to go to the principal's office. You know what that means, more time in the 'in-school suspension' room and a note to bring home about "Fighting" and "Failing."

* * * * *

A to F

When the ABCs of trauma happen over and over, the "F" for Failing starts to take over the "A" for Action.

"What happens" becomes:

"Everybody hates me"

"I can't win"

"I must be bad . . . No Good . . . and everybody knows it!"

It's as if the director of your movie, yells, "ACTION," but the same old story happens over and over. Every beginning starts to feel and look like an "F." Every day feels like a Failing day. Every feeling seems too much, too bad, and out of control. That's traumatic stress.

Trapped

When *tough times* keep happening over and over, it's easy to feel trapped. It may feel like you've fallen into a deep pit and it's beginning to rain. And, every time you feel yourself falling into the pit, the pit feels deeper and deeper. The worse you feel, the deeper the pit. Unfinished bad feelings make it harder and harder to get out of the pit.

That's when you start to feel trapped in a Trauma Pit. The bad feelings load you down, like rocks on top of your head, and tie you up like knots all the way up and down your body from your toes to your fingertips Your stomach starts to burn and your head may get so tight it aches.

Trapped[2]

Rage

Abandoned

Pressured

Pain

Emptiness

Defeated

Making Things Better

To get out of the Trauma Pit, you'll need to use all your power and grow stronger than all the bad feelings that are knocking you down.

To find a way out, it helps to know how you got in. It's just like a magic trick. When you know how it works, you own the power of the magic.

When bad things keep happening, you can use the *Power of Thinking* to make things better.

Action—What was one *tough time* that happened to you, something that made you feel just a *little* bit bad, like a "2" or "3" on the *Knots* scale? _____

_____

Body reactions—What was your first reaction? How did you feel the alarm bells going off in your body? ____

_____

What are some of the first clues inside your body when you have been reminded of *tough times*?_____

Catastrophic Thinking—When *tough times* happened, what did you think this meant about you? _____

"I thought I was: _____

Other people thought I was": _____

_____

Distress—How did your thoughts and beliefs make you feel inside? _____

How high were you on the *Knots* scale (1-10)? _____

How much *Personal Power* (1-10) did you have? _____

Emptiness—Did any one know how you felt? _____

Who could have helped? _____

_____

* * * * *

Life means regular days and special days; good times and not so good times. It takes courage to accept that:

Sometimes, bad things do happen, even to good people. In fact, bad things happen to everybody sooner or later.

What you felt, you felt. Feelings are messages from you body. They are not "bad" or "good," they are *just* feelings, the way your body learned to react to what happened in the past.

But, what you think and what you *do* is up to *you*.

You can fight failure by changing the story.

Changing the Story

You can become the director of your own story, just like the director of a movie. To change the story, release the Power of Your Thinking, the Power of your own mind. Then, you can change how the story goes.

You can find the script by taking a look at your beliefs:

Action—What happened, happened. Drawing what happened, putting it to music, acting it out as an *Action Pose,* and writing it down makes you the director and takes away the power of *tough times*. Try this out by drawing below, or on another sheet of paper, a picture of that same *tough time* when your *Knots* went up to a "2" or a "3."

What happened? _____

_____

_____

_____

✳ ✳ ✳ ✳ ✳

Bodily Reaction—How did your body feel? Draw a picture below (or on the back of this page) to show how you looked or take a photograph of yourself showing, in an *Action Pose,* how this felt.

Then, say how you felt in words: I felt ____________________________

____

* * * * *

In your new story, you can change the C of Catastrophic Thinking to C for Courage.

Courageous Thinking—What would help make things better?_____

If that happened, what would you think about yourself? I could _____

_____

Test out your thinking by taking a look at what you wrote four pages before about "I was . . ." Was this really true? Does believing this help or get in the way? What would you rather believe about yourself?

I am _____

I am good at: 1. _____ 2. _____

I like how I can: 1. _____ 2. _____

Check off each of the following beliefs that you would like to be true for you:

___I have been through tough times before and I can do it again

___I can help other people

___Deep down, I really do care about other people

___I have people who care about me

___Deep down, I know that I am a good person

Now, go back and put a double check mark for each of those beliefs that are already true for you.

✽ ✽ ✽ ✽ ✽

In your story, you can change the D from Distress to a D for Defeating Traumatic Stress. You can't change what happened in the past, but you can change how you cope and what you think and do.

Defeating Traumatic Stress—Some children remind themselves of people who love them by pulling out photographs or special gifts like a ring or a special stone. Some people learn to relax by taking deep breaths. Other children listen to a special song, walk in a special place, or remember a very special time when they felt safe and loved and peaceful.

What makes you feel better? I like to _____

_____

What can help you relax and lower your *Knots*? _____

_____

What helps you build your *Personal Power*?_____

_____

_____

✳ ✳ ✳ ✳ ✳

You can also change the E for Emptiness to an E for Excellence

Excellence—Who cared about you when you were little?

_____

Who cares about you now?_____

_____

Who will listen to you when you need to talk to someone?_____

_____

Who can give you good advice to make things better?_____

_____

Who can you help? _____ What could you do to help that person?_____

_____

* * * * *

Knowing how the ABCs work helps you build your skills and find solutions. Some skills may be hard to master. It takes practice, lots of practice, like learning to play an instrument or shooting a basket. But the more you practice, the better you get.

That's how you can change an F for Failing into an F for Freedom.

Freedom

Heroes know that being hurt is real. Bad things do happen. Sometimes good people get sick or get hurt or lose people they love. Heroes fight for FREEDOM from the bad times, and by so doing, make the world a little better for everyone.

You can choose FREEDOM[3] and DEFEAT TRAUMATIC STRESS:

Focus: Slow down, take a deep "belly" breath, center, and check your *Knots* and *Personal Power:*

This is how I focus myself: _____

_____

_____

Recognize my "triggers": the people, places, and things that remind me of my *tough times:*

These are the kind of *people* who look or sound or act like people who I lost or who hurt me or someone I loved: _____

_____

_____

These are some of the *places* that remind me of what I lost or where I was hurt or someone I loved was hurt: _____

_____

_____

These are some of the *things* that remind me of what I lost or where I was hurt or someone I loved was hurt: _____

_____

_____

Emotions: This is how I really feel: _____

_____

_____

Evaluate your thoughts

Here's what I really think about myself:

I am _____ (true/false).

If I could, I would change myself and then I would be _____

_____

Define what you really want, your true goals

This is my goal for today: _____

_____

This is my goal for this week: _____

_____

Options: This is what I will do to reach my goal: _____

_____

I can get help from _____

_____

Make the world a little bit better:

This is what I can do:_____

_____

_____

✳ ✳ ✳ ✳ ✳

Now comes the tricky part. You see, saying it, even writing it down, isn't enough. You have to do it.

And, just like learning to make a winning jump shot or play a guitar, it takes practice. It's like learning to ride a bike. At first, to a little child, it seems impossible, but then, with a lot of practice and a helpful guide, it suddenly clicks. That's when the magic happens.

After you have worked on winning your own FREEDOM, then you're ready to move ahead with the Hero's Challenge.

The Hero's Challenge

Every hero story begins with someone who has been hurt, a boy or a girl, a man or a woman. Wounds can make us stronger or weaker, like scars. Scar tissue is tough. But unhealed wounds mean that the infection is still there.

Heroes muster the courage to heal from their wounds and use what they learn to help others who must face the same *tough times*.

Healing means using the pain in our lives to grow stronger instead of running away, lashing out at others, or hurting ourselves.

Emotions are natural. Celebrate them, use them to develop strength. To find your true feelings, take time to center yourself and check what is real.

Release the power of your own thinking; evaluate your beliefs and change from Catastrophic to Courageous Thinking.

Open up options: What do you need and want? How would other heroes solve this problem? Who would you want to help you? Real life heroes need friends, teachers, coaches, and mentors.

Experiment: Muster the courage to check out and test out new solutions. Courage can be learned but it takes practice. Skills take practice, but we can all learn. Mistakes mean we're learning.

Stronger and **S**tronger: Find your skills and build them. Remember who cared about you in the past and find people who care enough to help you grow—people who won't knock you down. Move from strength to strength to help yourself and other people.

* * * * *

If you are ready for the Hero's Challenge, it's time to go to Chapter 7 of your *Real Life Heroes* book.

* * *

NOTES

1. Ford, J. D., & Russo, E. (2006). A trauma-focused, present-centered, emotional self-regulation approach to integrated treatment for post-traumatic stress and addiction: Trauma adaptive recovery group education therapy (TARGET). *American Journal of Psychotherapy.*

2. Ibid.

3. Ibid.

Chapter 25

Resource Checklist

Service Providers

_____ Recognize and respect family strengths, caring for child, and ethnic heritage as well as the impact of any violence, abuse, neglect, losses, or hardships

_____ Demystify children's behaviors including predictable reactions to the difficult work of overcoming trauma, the need to grieve losses, and the pulls and pressures to repeat traumatic experiences

_____ Engage and contract, wherever possible, to work with parents, extended family, caretakers, children, and other therapists to change trauma cycles for the good of all, utilizing psychoeducation on trauma to replace any shaming and pathologizing with positive steps toward creating safety, building strengths, and fostering enduring positive attachments

_____ Practice *and* test strength and viability of safety plans for children, caring adults, and for themselves

_____ Develop back-up plans for rebuilding attachments if child's primary caretakers become unable or unwilling to raise child

Caring Adults: Parents, Guardians, or Primary Caretakers

_____ Understand impact of trauma on children's neurophysiological development and behavior as well as how caring adults can help children rebuild trust and learn new behavioral patterns

_____ Demonstrate and encourage use of creative arts and words to express feelings, beliefs, and memories

_____ Modulate own anxiety, anger, and impulses well enough to protect child from becoming overwhelmed or feeling they must "parent" adults or protect adults from facing traumas

_____ Develop, implement, and practice safety plans for self and children

_____ Accept and acknowledge validity of children's experiences

Children

_____ Understand at age-appropriate level how traumas including neglect and family violence lead to natural reactions including hyperarousal, agitation, startle responses, hypervigilance, avoidance, and reexperiencing past sensory experiences (auditory, smell, tactile, visual, motor) in the present as flashbacks

_____ Understand how reminders of past traumas trigger repetitions of trauma reactions—the *ABCs of Trauma*

Real Life Heroes: Practitioner's Manual
Published by The Haworth Press, Inc., 2007. All rights reserved.
doi:10.1300/5639_31

_____ Demonstrate age-appropriate skills to:
— Identify and express basic feelings
— Self-monitor how feeling states change (*Knots* and *Personal Power* Thermometers) without immediate fear/flight/fight responses
— Differentiate internal reactions (e.g., hyperarousal) from outside precipitating events
— Express thoughts, actions, and feelings for memories
— Associate words with feelings and think about what is happening
— Utilize calming messages, imagery, and movement to reduce stress, e.g., "SOS" and deep breathing
— Remind self of goals and use self-talk to guide behavior
— Reduce blaming and shaming of self and others
— Focus on one step at a time when working on an activity
— Reinforce themselves for small achievements
— Recognize triggers and alarm signals in their bodies and work to calm self without dangerous reenactments of trauma cycles
— Manage frustrations and modulate anger and fear sufficiently to avoid harm to themselves or others

References

Abbuhl, J. (2006, February 15). Personal communication.

Achenbach, T. & Rescoria, L. (2000a). Child Behavior Checklist 1 1/2—5. Burlington, VT: ASEBA, University of Vermont.

Achenbach, T. & Rescoria, L. (2000b). Child Behavior Checklist 6—18. Burlington, VT: ASEBA, University of Vermont.

Alexander, D.W. (1993a). *All My Dreams.* Creative Healing Book Series. Plainview, NY: The Bureau for At-Risk Youth.

Alexander, D.W. (1993b). *It Happened in Autumn.* Creative Healing Book Series. Plainview, NY: The Bureau for At-Risk Youth.

Alexander, D.W. (1993c). *It's My Life.* Creative Healing Book Series. Plainview, NY: The Bureau for At-Risk Youth.

Alexander, D.W. (1993d). *When I Remember.* Creative Healing Book Series. Plainview, NY: The Bureau for At-Risk Youth.

Austin, D. (2002). The wounded healer: The voice of trauma: A wounded healer's perspective. In Julie Sutton (Ed.), *Music, Music Therapy and Trauma: International Perspectives.* Philadelphia: Jessica Kingsley Publishers.

Beck, A.T. (1976) *Cognitive Therapy and the Emotional Disorders.* New York: International Universities Press.

Becker-Weidman, A. (2002, May 17). Understanding attachment disorder: The broken bond. Workshop presentation. Albany, New York.

Benamati, J. (2004). *Systematic Training to Assist in the Recovery from Trauma (S.T.A.R.T.): A Trauma Informed Curriculum for Residential Childcare Workers.* Albany, NY: Parsons Child and Family Center.

Berliner, L. (2004). Workshop Introduction. Family Violence and Sexual Assault Institute, San Diego, CA.

Black, C. (1984). *The Story Game: A Game of Feelings.* Bainbridge Island, WA: MAC Publishing

Blaustein, M. (2006). Interview from *Treating Children with Disrupted Attachment.* Nevada City, CA: Cavalcade Productions

Bloom, S. (1997). *Creating Sanctuary: Toward the Evolution of Sane Societies.* New York: Routledge.

Briere, J. (1996). *Trauma Symptom Checklist for Children.* Lutz, FL: Psychological Assessment Resources, Inc.

Brown, C. (2005). Personal communication.

Campbell, J. (1968). *The Hero with a Thousand Faces.* Princeton, N.J.: Princeton University Press.

Casebeer Art Productions (1989). *Projective Storytelling Cards.* Reading, CA: Northwest Psychological Publishers.

Cloitre, M., Koenen, K., Cohen, L., & Han, H. (2002). Skill training in affective and interpersonal regulation followed by exposure: A phase-based treatment for PTSD related to childhood abuse. *Journal of Consulting Clinical Psychology,* 70(5): 1067-1074.

Cloitre, M., Koenen, K.C., & Cohen, L.R. (2006). *Treating Survivors of Childhood Abuse: Psychotherapy for the Interrupted Life.* New York: Guilford.

Cohen, J.A., Deblinger, E., & Mannarino, A.P. (2006). *Treating Trauma and Traumatic Grief in Children and Adolescents.* New York: Guilford.

Real Life Heroes: Practitioner's Manual
Published by The Haworth Press, Inc., 2007. All rights reserved.
doi:10.1300/5639_32

Cohen, J.A., Greenberg, T., Padlo, S., Shipley, C., Mannarino, A.P., Deblinger, E., & Stubenbort, K. (2001). Cognitive behavioral therapy for traumatic bereavement in children treatment manual. Pittsburgh, PA: Allegheny General Hospital.

Cohen, J.A., Mannarino, A.P., & Deblinger, E. (2003). Child and parent trauma-focused cognitive behavioral therapy treatment manual. Unpublished Manuscript. Pittsburgh, PA: Allegheny General Hospital.

Conners, C.K. (1997). *Conners Parent Rating Scales-Revised* (Long Version). North Tonawanda, NY: Multi-Health Systems, Inc.

Cook, A., Blaustein, M., Spinazzola, J., & van der Kolk, B. (Eds.) (2003). Complex trauma in children and adolescents: White paper from the National Child Traumatic Stress Network Complex Trauma Task Force. Los Angeles, CA: National Center for Child Traumatic Stress (www.NCTSNet.org)

Cook, D. (2005). Personal communication.

Cunningham, C. (1992). *All Kinds of Separation.* Indianapolis: Kidsrights

Deblinger, E. (2005). Personal communication. TF-CBT consultations (2/9/05).

Deblinger, E. & Heflin, A.H. (1996). *Treating Sexually Abused Children and Their Non-Offending Parents: A Cognitive Behavioral Approach.* Thousand Oaks: Sage.

DeRosa, R.R., Pelcovitz, D., Kaplan, S., Rathus, J., Ford, J., Layne, C., & Saltzman, W. (2005). *Structured Psychotherapy for Adolescents Responding to Chronic Stress (SPARCS).* Manhasset, NY: North Shore University Hospital.

Dolan, Y. (1991). *Resolving Sexual Abuse.* New York: Norton.

Eggert, L.L. (1994). *Anger Management for Youth: Stemming Aggression and Violence.* Bloomington, IN: National Educational Service.

Evans, M.D (1986). *This Is Me and My Two Families.* New York: Magination Press.

Figley, C. (1989). *Helping Traumatized Families.* San Francisco: Jossey-Bass.

Fisher, A., Abarquez, A., Kitowski, C., & Sims, L. (2005). CAPS: Collaborative Advanced Preparation Skills: Curriculum and trainer's guide. Houston, Texas: DePelchin Children's Center (Unpublished manuscript).

Ford, J., Mahoney, K., & Russo, E. (2001). *TARGET and FREEDOM (for children).* Farmington, CT: University of Connecticut Health Center.

Ford, J.D., Mahoney, K., & Russo, E. (2003). *TARGET Trauma Adaptive Recovery Group Education and Therapy (9 Session Version) Leader Guide and Participant Handouts.* Farmington, CT: University of Connecticut Health Center. (Note: Includes current handouts from TARGET-AR/AT Trauma Adaptive Recovery Group Education and Therapy; Parent Education: Understanding how trauma affects parents and children.)

Ford, J.D. & Russo, E. (2006). A trauma-focused, present-centered, emotional self-regulation approach to integrated treatment for post-traumatic stress and addiction: Trauma adaptive recovery group education and therapy (TARGET). *American Journal of Psychotherapy.*

Ford, J. & St. Juste, M.C. (2006). *TARGET-A: Trauma Affect Regulation: Guide for Education and Therapy.* Farmington, CT: University of Connecticut (see www.ptsdfreedom.org).

Freedman, J. & Combs, G. (1996). *Narrative Therapy: The Social Construction of Preferred Realities.* New York: Norton.

Gardner, R. (1975). *Psychotherapeutic Approaches to the Resistant Child.* New York: Jason Aronson.

Greenwald, R. (1999). *Eye Movement Desensitization and Reprocessing (EMDR) in Child and Adolescent Psychotherapy.* Northvale, NJ: Jason Aronson.

Greenwald, R. & Rubin, A. (1999a). Brief assessment of childrens post-traumatic symptoms: Development and preliminary validation of parent and child scales. *Research on Social Work Practice, 9,* 61-75.

Greenwald R. & Rubin, A. (1999b). *Child Report of Post-Traumatic Symptoms/Parent Report of Post-Traumatic Symptoms (CROPS/PROPS).* Baltimore, MD: Sidran Institute.

Herman, J. (1992). *Trauma and Recovery.* New York: Basic Books.

Hughes, D. (1997). *Facilitating Developmental Attachment.* Northvale, NJ: Jason Aronson.

Hughes, D. (1998, March 18). Working with attachment disorder: From frustration to hope. Conference presentation, Albany, New York.

James, B. (1989). *Treating Traumatized Children.* Lexington, MA: Lexington Books.

James, B. (1994). *Handbook for Treatment of Attachment-Trauma Problems in Children.* New York: Lexington.

Jessie (1991). *Please Tell.* Center City, MN: Hazeldon Foundation.

Jewett, C. (1978). *Adopting the Older Child.* Cambridge, MA: The Harvard Common Press.

Kabat-Zinn, J. (1990). *Full Catastrophe Living: How to Cope with Stress, Pain and Illness Using Mindfulness Meditation.* New York: Delacorte.

Kagan, L. (2005). Personal communication.

Kagan, R. (1996). *Turmoil to Turning Points: Building Hope for Children in Crisis Placements.* New York: Norton.

Kagan, R. (2003). *Wounded Angels: Lessons of Courage from Children in Crisis.* Washington, DC: Children's Press, Child Welfare League of America.

Kagan, R. (2004a). *Real Life Heroes: A Life Sorybook for Children.* Binghamton, NY: The Haworth Press.

Kagan, R. (2004b). *Rebuilding Attachments with Traumatized Children: Healing from Losses, Violence, Abuse, and Neglect.* Binghamton, NY: The Haworth Press.

Kagan, R., Douglas, A., Hornik, J., & Kratz, S. (in press). *Real Life Heroes Pilot Study: Evaluation of a Treatment Model for Children with Traumatic Stress. Journal of Child and Adolescent Trauma.*

Kagan, R. & Schlosberg, S. (1989). *Families in Perpetual Crisis.* New York: Norton.

Kerns, K., Klepac, L., & Cole, A. (1996). Peer relationships and preadolescents' perceptions of security in the child-mother relationship. *Developmental Psychology, 32,* 457-466.

Kliman, G.W. (1996). *The Personal Life Historybook Method: A Manual for Preventive Psychotherapy with Foster Children.* San Francisco, CA: The Children's Psychological Trauma Center.

Kolko, D. & Swenson, C.C. (2002). *Assessing and Treating Physically Abused Children and Their Families.* Thousand Oaks, CA: Sage.

Layne, C.M., Saltzman, W.S., Savjak, N., & Pynoos, R.S. (1999). *Trauma/Grief-Focused Group Psychotherapy Manual.* Sarajevo, Bosnia: UNICEF Bosnia & Herzegovina.

Lazarus, A. (1971). *Behavior Therapy and Beyond.* New York: McGraw-Hill Book Company.

Lee, S. (1963). *The Amazing Spider-Man.* New York, NY: Marvel Enterprises, Inc.

Macy, R. (2004). Annual Meeting, National Child Traumatic Stress Network, San Diego.

Macy, R. D., Barry, S., & Gil, N.G. (2003). *Youth Facing Threat and Terror: Supporting Preparedness and Resilience.* San Francisco: Jossey-Bass.

Madanes, C. (1990). *Sex, Love, and Violence: Strategies for Transformation.* New York: Norton.

Mahoney, K., Ford, J. D., & Cruz, St. Juste M. C. (2005). *TARGET-A: Trauma Adaptive Recovery Group Education and Therapy (10+ Session Adolescent Version) Facilitator Guide.* Farmington, CT: University of Connecticut Health Center.

Miller, A.L., Rathus, J.H., & Linehan, M.M. (2006). *Dialectical Behavior Therapy for Suicidal Adolescents.* Guilford Press.

Miller, W.I. (2002). *The Mystery of Courage.* Cambridge, MA: Harvard University Press.

Mitlin, M. (1998). *Emotional Bingo.* Los Angeles: Western Psychological Services.

Mormile, A. (2005). Personal communication.

Mullin, S. (2000). Personal communication.

Mullin, S. (2004). Personal communication.

Munson, L. & Riskin, K. (1995). *In Their Own Words: A Sexual Abuse Workbook for Teenage Girls.* Washington DC: Child Welfare League of America.

Nadeau, K.G. & Dixon, E.B. (1997). *Learning to Slow Down and Pay Attention: A Book for Kids About ADD.* Washington, DC: Magination Press.

O'Conner, J.J. (1983). Color your life techniques. In C.E. Schaefer & J.J. O'Connor (Eds.), *Handbook of Play Therapy.* New York: Wiley.

Ogden, P., Minton, K., & Pain, C. (in press). *Trauma and the Body: The Theory and Practice of Sensorimotor psychotherapy.* New York: W.W. Norton.

Peacock, C. & Hawkins, C. (2004). Personal communication.

Peak Potential, Inc. (1999). *The Mad, Sad, Glad, Game.* Fort Collins, CO: Peak Potential, Inc.

Perry, B.D. & Pollard, R. (1998). Homeostasis, stress, trauma, and adaptation: A neurodevelopmental view of childhood trauma. *Child and Adolescent Psychiatric Clinics of North America, 7,* 33-51.

Pitman, R.K., Altman, B., Greenwald, E., Longpre, R.E, et al. (1991). Psychiatric complications during flooding therapy for posttraumatic stress disorder. *Journal of Clinical Psychiatry, 52,* 17-20.

Purdy, M. (2003). Personal communication.

Purdy, M. (2004). Personal communication.

Pynoos, R.S. & Nader, K. (1988). Psychological first aid and treatment approach to children exposed to community violence. *Journal of Traumatic Stress,* 1, 445-471.

Pynoos,R., Rodriquez, N., Steinberg, A., Stuber, M., & Frederick, C. (1998). *UCLA PTSD Index for DSM IV.* Los Angeles, CA: UCLA Trauma Psychiatry Service.

Pynoos, R.S. & Steinberg, A.M. (2004). Recovery of children and adolescents after exposure to violence: A developmental ecological framework. Paper presented at the Johnson and Johnson Pediatric Round Table "Children Exposed to Violence," San Juan, Puerto Rico.

Rappaport, S. (2006). Personal communication.

Roberts, G.E. (n.d.). Roberts Appreciation Test. Los Angeles: Western Psychological Services.

Rojano, R. (1998, October 9). Community family therapy. Workshop presented at the Sidney Albert Institute Fall Institute, Albany, New York.

Rothbaum, B. & Schwartz, A. (2002). Exposure therapy for posttraumatic stress disorder. *American Journal of Psychotherapy,* 56 (1): 59-75.

Saltzman, W.R., Layne, C.M., & Pynoos, R.S. (2003). *Trauma/Grief-Focused Group Psychotherapy: Supplementary Materials.* Unpublished treatment manual, University of California, Los Angeles.

Scheele, A. (2005). Personal communication.

Schore, A.N. (2003). Early relational trauma, disorganized attachment, and the development of a predisposition to violence. In M.F. Solomon & D.J. Siegel (Eds.), *Healing Trauma: Attachment, Mind, Body, and Brain.* New York: Norton.

Shapiro, F. (2001). *Eye Movement Desensitization and Reprocessing: Basic Principles, Protocols, and Procedures* (Second Edition). New York: Guilford Press.

Siegel, D. (1999). *The Developing Mind.* New York: Guilford Press.

Siegel, D. & Hartzell, M. (2003). *Parenting from the Inside Out: How a Deeper Self-Understanding Can Help You Raise Children Who Thrive.* New York: JP Tarcher/Putnam.

Sutton, P. (2004) Personal communication.

Tinker, R.H. & Wilson, S.A. (1999) *Through the Eyes of a Child: EMDR with Children.* New York: Norton.

van der Kolk, B. (2003). Posttraumatic stress disorder and the nature of trauma. In M.F. Solomon & D.J. Siegel (Eds.), *Healing Trauma: Attachment, Mind, Body, and Brain.* New York: Norton.

van der Kolk, B. (2005). Developmental trauma disorder. *Psychiatric Annals,* 35(5): 401-409.

van Gulden, H. & Bartels-Robb, L.M. (1995). *Real Parents, Real Children: Parenting the Adopted Child.* New York: Crossroads.

Vogler, C. (1998). *The Writer's Journey: Mythic Structure for Writers.* Studio City, CA: Michael Weise Production.

Walk, R.D. (1956). Self-ratings of fear in a fear-involving situation. *Journal of Abnormal and Social Psychology,* 52, 171-178.

White, M. & Epston, D. (1990). *Narrative Means to Therapeutic Ends.* New York: Norton.

Whitehouse, E. & Pudney,W. (1996). *A Volcano in My Tummy.* Gabriola Island, BC: New Society Publishers.

Wolfelt, A. (1991). Children. *Bereavement Magazine,* 5(1): 38-39.

Index

Real Life Heroes: Practitioner's Manual
Published by The Haworth Press, Inc., 2007. All rights reserved.
doi:10.1300/5639_33